Assessing Tax Compliance and Illicit Financial Flows in South Africa

This work is published under the responsibility of the Secretary-General of the OECD. The opinions expressed and arguments employed herein do not necessarily reflect the official views of the Member countries of the OECD.

This document, as well as any data and map included herein, are without prejudice to the status of or sovereignty over any territory, to the delimitation of international frontiers and boundaries and to the name of any territory, city or area.

The statistical data for Israel are supplied by and under the responsibility of the relevant Israeli authorities. The use of such data by the OECD is without prejudice to the status of the Golan Heights, East Jerusalem and Israeli settlements in the West Bank under the terms of international law.

Note by Turkey
The information in this document with reference to "Cyprus" relates to the southern part of the Island. There is no single authority representing both Turkish and Greek Cypriot people on the Island. Turkey recognises the Turkish Republic of Northern Cyprus (TRNC). Until a lasting and equitable solution is found within the context of the United Nations, Turkey shall preserve its position concerning the "Cyprus issue".

Note by all the European Union Member States of the OECD and the European Union
The Republic of Cyprus is recognised by all members of the United Nations with the exception of Turkey. The information in this document relates to the area under the effective control of the Government of the Republic of Cyprus.

Please cite this publication as:
OECD (2022), *Assessing Tax Compliance and Illicit Financial Flows in South Africa*, OECD Publishing, Paris, https://doi.org/10.1787/e8c9ff5b-en.

ISBN 978-92-64-74644-2 (print)
ISBN 978-92-64-60236-6 (pdf)
ISBN 978-92-64-98169-0 (HTML)
ISBN 978-92-64-34491-4 (epub)

Photo credits: Cover © Exeter_Acres/Shutterstock.com.

Corrigenda to publications may be found on line at: www.oecd.org/about/publishing/corrigenda.htm.
© OECD 2022

The use of this work, whether digital or print, is governed by the Terms and Conditions to be found at https://www.oecd.org/termsandconditions.

Foreword

This study was produced by the Tax Policy and Statistics Division of the OECD's Centre for Tax Policy and Administration (CTPA). It is the first product of a joint project between the OECD's Centre for Tax Policy and Administration and the National Treasury of South Africa to analyse illicit financial flows (IFFs) in South Africa. Whilst this study provides an estimate of IFFs, and thereafter focuses on tax-related IFFs given the availability of tax-data, further studies could analyse non-tax IFFs, in line with the broader objectives of the joint project. Whilst the studies reflect the views of the authors, they do not necessarily reflect the views of National Treasury, and are intended to lay the basis for further research and evidence to guide policy responses to illicit financial flows.

The joint project team overseeing the project consists of Errol Makhubela (National Treasury), Pierce O'Reilly (OECD), Varsha Singh (ATAF), and Michael A. Stemmer (OECD). The analysis was carried out and coordinated by Michael A. Stemmer. The report was drafted by Michael A. Stemmer under the supervision of Pierce O'Reilly. Chris Axelson from the National Treasury contributed to the analysis of CRS data featured in Chapter 6.

The authors would like to thank David Bradbury for his guidance and feedback throughout the project. The authors are also very grateful to Carrie Tyler, Natalie Lagorce, Hazel Healy and Karena Garnier for their support with communications and formatting, and to Violet Sochay, Marie-Aurélie Elkurd and Alexandra Le Cam, for their assistance with administrative matters. The authors would also like to thank Andrew Auerbach, Nilimesh Baruah, Winfrid Blaschke, Bert Brys, Céline Colin, Melissa Dejong, Ben Dickinson, Falilou Fall, Peter Green, Hakim Hamadi, Paul Hondius, Radhanath Housden, Philip Kerfs, Gwenaëlle Le Coustumer, Marcos Roca, Joseph Stead, Ervice Tchouata, and participants in CTPA's Brownbag Lunch Seminar for helpful comments and suggestions.

In addition to OECD colleagues, the authors would like to acknowledge the very helpful input and support received from Chris Axelson and Hayley Erasmus from the National Treasury and Godfrey Baloyi, Johan George Fourie, Thembile Hlati and Thabile Ntombela from the South Africa Revenue Service, Annet Wanyana Oguttu from the University of Pretoria, Steve Dawe from the International Monetary Fund, and Pierre Bardin from the Financial Action Task Force. The authors would like to particularly thank Carel Lombard from the South Africa Revenue Service for his assistance in preparing the data used for the study.

This report was produced with the financial assistance of the governments of Ireland, Japan, Luxembourg, the Netherlands, Norway, Sweden, Switzerland and the United Kingdom. The contents of the report do not necessarily reflect the official opinion of any of these governments.

Table of contents

Foreword	3
Abbreviations and acronyms	7
Executive summary	9
1 Overview	**11**
References	13
2 Macroeconomic and fiscal context in South Africa	**14**
Macroeconomic environment	14
Fiscal environment	19
Impact of COVID-19	22
Conclusion	26
References	27
Notes	28
3 IFFs in the global and South African context	**29**
Introduction	29
Defining IFFs	29
Why are IFFs so harmful?	32
Existing IFF estimates and measurement challenges	32
Risks and sources of IFFs in South Africa	34
South Africa's multilateral action against tax-related IFFs	36
Domestic tax transparency initiatives in South Africa	39
References	42
Notes	44
4 The tax system in South Africa	**46**
Introduction	46
An overview of the South African tax system	46
Income taxes in South Africa	47
References	51
Notes	51
5 Taxpayer responses to increasing tax transparency in South Africa	**52**
Introduction	52
Data	54

Methodology	56
Evidence on tax compliance from tax returns data	56
Taxpayer responsiveness to domestic tax transparency initiatives	61
Results and policy implications	70
References	72
Notes	73

6 Assessing the size of undeclared foreign wealth and IFFs through the CRS 75

Introduction	75
Overview of South African CRS data	76
The importance of IFC accounts in South Africa's CRS data	77
Income tax compliance analysed through the CRS	80
Estimating past non-compliant offshore wealth and IFFs from tax data	83
Results and policy implications	91
References	92
Notes	94

7 Summary and key recommendations 95

| References | 97 |

FIGURES

Figure 2.1. Annual GDP growth across different regions during 2010 - 20	15
Figure 2.2. Challenges in well-being and inequality	16
Figure 2.3. Contributions to investment growth on the decline	17
Figure 2.4. FDI and portfolio flows in South Africa	18
Figure 2.5. Debt and debt-service costs in South Africa	20
Figure 2.6. Debt trajectories in South Africa	21
Figure 2.7. Tax-to-GDP ratios in selected regions, 2009 to 2018	21
Figure 2.8. COVID-19 and economic growth impact	23
Figure 2.9. COVID-19 and South Africa's fiscal picture	24
Figure 2.10. The impact of COVID-19 on the labour market	25
Figure 2.11. The onset of COVID-19 resulted in pronounced reversal of capital flows	26
Figure 3.1. UN Categorisation of IFFs	30
Figure 3.2. Landmarks of tax transparency in South Africa over time	37
Figure 3.3. The expansion of South Africa's EOIR network over time, 1956 – 2019	38
Figure 4.1. The tax mix in South Africa compared to African and OECD countries in 2018	47
Figure 4.2. Net changes in tax-to-GDP ratios for South Africa and selected countries, 2010 - 2019	48
Figure 4.3. Income tax plus employees' and employers' social security contributions, 2019	49
Figure 4.4. Tax trends in South Africa over time	50
Figure 5.1. The number of individuals reporting foreign interest income peaks in 2014	57
Figure 5.2. The number of individuals reporting foreign dividends income peaks in 2014	58
Figure 5.3. The number of individuals reporting foreign capital gains increases over time	58
Figure 5.4. New tax reports for foreign incomes spike in 2014 and 2017	59
Figure 5.5. Total foreign income reporting is different for old and new tax return filers	60
Figure 5.6. Reporting with respect to foreign capital income also shows a distinct pattern for new filers	61
Figure 5.7. SVDP applications peak before AEOI commencement	62
Figure 5.8. Jurisdictions of offshore trusts and their effective management	64
Figure 5.9. Offshore locations of investments in other financial assets	64
Figure 5.10. Average wealth hidden abroad per jurisdiction and asset class	65
Figure 5.11. VDP applications over time	66
Figure 5.12. VDP applications by tax type	67
Figure 5.13. Tax evasion over time by dual SVDP-VDP applicants	68
Figure 5.14. The top income levels hold a majority share of total SVDP offshore wealth	69
Figure 5.15. Main source of income for SVDP/VDP applicants and non-applicants	70

Figure 6.1. IFCs dominate account balances 78
Figure 6.2. IFCs dominate account balances of individuals and corporates 79
Figure 6.3. Non-IFCs and IFCs differ in financial services provided 80
Figure 6.4. Tax number availability and matching rates across jurisdictions 81
Figure 6.5. Comparison of foreign capital income declarations with CRS account payments 82
Figure 6.6. Middle-high income individuals predominantly declared foreign capital income 83
Figure 6.7. Previously non-compliant offshore wealth imputed from returns by new tax filers 85
Figure 6.8. The high frequency of IFC jurisdictions in SVDP and CRS data 86
Figure 6.9. Estimating hitherto undeclared offshore wealth from CRS accounts 87
Figure 6.10. Estimates of annual IFF outflows 89
Figure 6.11. Sensitivity analysis to IFF estimates 90

TABLES

Table 5.1. Hidden offshore wealth declared in the SVDP 63
Table 6.1. Summary statistics 76
Table 6.2. Total payments received by type 77

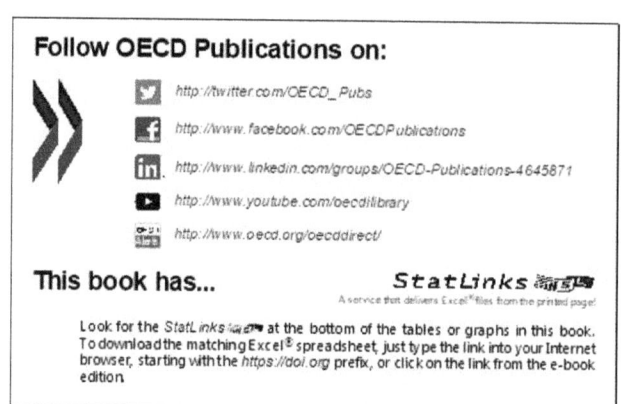

Abbreviations and acronyms

AEOI	Automatic Exchange of Information
ATAF	African Tax Administration Forum
AMATM	African Tax Administration Forum Agreement on Mutual Assistance in Tax Matters
BRICS	Brazil, Russia, India, China, and South Africa
CMA	Common Monetary Area
CRS	Common Reporting Standard
CLCM	Code of Liberalisation of Capital Movements
EOI	Exchange of Information
EOIR	Exchange of Information on Request
FATF	Financial Action Task Force
FDI	Foreign Direct Investment
GDP	Gross Domestic Product
HNWI	High Net Wealth Individuals
IFC	International Financial Centre
IFF	Illicit Financial Flows
MAAC	Convention on Mutual Administrative Assistance in Tax Matters
MCAA	Multilateral Competent Authority Agreement
MLI	Multilateral Instrument
NT	National Treasury
SADC	Southern African Development Community
SADCA	Southern African Development Community Cooperation in Accreditation
SARB	South Africa Reserve Bank
SARS	South Africa National Treasury
SSCs	Social Security Contributions
SVDP	Special Voluntary Disclosure Programme
USD	United States Dollars
UNODC	United Nations Office on Drugs and Crime

UNCTAD	United Nations Conference on Trade and Development
VAT	Value-Added Tax
VDP	Voluntary Disclosure Programme
ZAR	South African Rand

Executive summary

This report is the product of a joint project between the OECD's Centre for Tax Policy and Administration and the National Treasury of South Africa to analyse illicit financial flows (IFFs) in South Africa. This study considers that IFFs comprise cross-border financial flows that are illegal in origin, transfer or use, and therefore do not include tax avoidance. While the study measures all IFFs the policy discussion focuses on tax-related IFFs, noting that non-tax related IFFs could be more significant. Using new taxpayer microdata, including anonymised data exchanged under the Common Reporting Standard (CRS) and information collected under South Africa's voluntary disclosure programmes (VDPs), the study quantifies the scale of non-tax-compliant assets held abroad by South Africans, and sheds new light on taxpayer responses to global and domestic tax transparency initiatives.

IFFs pose a major threat to many developing and emerging economies, as they undermine domestic resource mobilisation efforts. In the context of relatively narrow tax bases and constrained tax administration capacity, IFFs erode the public revenues that countries need to invest in their social and economic development. Apart from their damaging effects on public revenues, IFFs can also erode the investment base of countries and undermine the public's confidence in the integrity of the tax system.

The report finds that IFFs continue to represent a significant challenge for South Africa, with the analysis estimating that between USD 3.5 and 5 billion in IFFs are leaving the country each year. This estimate, which represents approximately 1-1.5% of South African annual GDP, is derived from estimates of between USD 40 and 54 billion in hidden South African-owned assets held in international financial centres (IFCs) in 2018. These figures may also reflect the impact of state capture in South Africa during 2009-18, including the deliberate weakening of the South African Revenue Services during 2014-18, as evidenced by the dismantling of its Large Business Centre and removing top management (as noted in the first part of the report of the Judicial Commission of Inquiry into Allegations of State Capture chaired by Judge Zondo).

IFFs are particularly harmful in South Africa due to the significant fiscal challenges that the country faces. These stem from low growth in the past, rising debt levels, and socio-economic challenges such as high rates of poverty, labour market informality and unemployment, as well as the strain placed on South Africa by the COVID-19 pandemic. Against this backdrop, more effective efforts to curtail IFFs and combat tax evasion will be needed as part of South Africa's overall fiscal strategy.

While IFFs are inherently secret and therefore difficult to measure, this study adopts a novel approach that is based on CRS data, which is a new, more granular and country-specific data source. Many prior studies have focussed on errors and omissions in global macroeconomic statistics, which risks conflating measurement errors with IFFs, and may lead to biased and enlarged estimates. Unlike other approaches, in this paper the estimates of IFFs are based on the assumptions that IFFs from South Africa are not tax-compliant, regardless of the type of flow (e.g. smuggling, illicit trade, or corruption), and that these flows are likely to end up in financial accounts in IFCs. These two assumptions together allow the use of the stocks of foreign wealth reported under the CRS to estimate all IFFs of various kinds leaving South Africa over recent years.

New taxpayer data, including from VDPs highlights that tax evasion has a long history in South Africa and that most of it has been concentrated among the very wealthy. VDP applications suggest that taxpayers evaded taxes on average for about 10 years, with the largest share of hidden wealth declared through these programmes belonging to top income recipients.

Transparency initiatives, such as the CRS and domestic VDPs have played an important role in South Africa's efforts to date to tackle IFFs. The study presents evidence that the expansion of information exchange has produced significant taxpayer behavioural responses, with some taxpayers declaring their hidden wealth for the first time. Under South Africa's special VDP, 375 taxpayers reported a total of USD 349 million, which has resulted in the payment of an additional USD 30 million in taxes. Importantly, a significant spike in the numbers of taxpayers declaring previously undeclared wealth is observed immediately before the commencement of the Automatic Exchange of Information (AEOI). In addition, the analysis of tax return data suggests that a further USD 20 million may have been disclosed in the form of 'soft disclosures', where a taxpayer increases taxes paid without formally participating in a VDP.

While these results represent important steps in the right direction, more needs to be done to improve tax compliance and more effectively address IFFs in South Africa. While the exchange of taxpayer information (EOI) and the use of VDPs has helped improved tax compliance, the report makes a number of concrete recommendations on how South Africa can tackle IFFs more effectively in the future. For example, the report recommends:

- **Improved analytical capacities**: in the tax authority to make better use of CRS data is identified as a key priority.
- **An increase in the use of existing EOI treaties for requesting information held abroad on specific taxpayers:** particularly with well-known IFCs, should be pursued.
- **Better use of exchanged information and improved matching of CRS data with taxpayer records**. South Africa could make better use of Exchange of Information on Request to follow up on information exchanged through AEOI, with only a small number of requests currently being sent to partners each year. Assistance provided through Tax Inspectors Without Borders (TIWB) could be helpful in this regard, with TIWB now providing experts to directly help interpret and analyse data exchanged for tax purposes on a confidential basis.
- **Enhanced collaboration and augmented data sharing across relevant authorities**: is needed to strengthen analytical and enforcement efforts, including through the onward sharing of CRS data with other law enforcement agencies. The OECD's Fighting Tax Crime – The Ten Global Principles, provides a useful framework for South Africa and other countries to gauge progress against fighting tax crimes. It sets out ten essential principles covering the legal, institutional, administrative, and operational aspects necessary for developing an efficient and effective system for identifying, investigating and prosecuting tax crimes, while respecting the rights of accused taxpayers.

The report also highlights that ongoing analysis of IFFs is crucial to understanding them better. This study, which utilises new data sources on cross-border financial accounts, contends that further analysis based on CRS data offers a credible and robust methodology for estimating IFFs, and suggests that studies such as the present one could be replicated for a range of developing and emerging economies in the future to help tackle IFFs and boost domestic resource mobilisation.

1 Overview

South Africa faces significant fiscal challenges due to the ongoing COVID-19 pandemic. During the 1990s and early 2000s, South Africa saw significant improvements in economic development, per capita income and overall well-being. In the aftermath of the global financial crisis, however, the country has been faced with sustained low growth, rising debt levels and socio-economic challenges such as high poverty, inequality and unemployment rates, which have resulted in limited fiscal space. While the situation was already difficult before, the COVID-19 pandemic has exacerbated these issues with the country's gross domestic product (GDP) contracting by 6.4% in 2020. To alleviate its impact, the government's implementation of fiscal measures has been rapid and comprehensive, deploying emergency liquidity provisions and financial support of more than 10% of 2020 GDP. While these measures have helped to cushion the detrimental effects on the economy and public health, making public finances more resilient and returning to a more sustainable fiscal path in the future will require sizeable additional financial efforts. Moreover, achieving the sustainable development goals (SDGs) by 2030 further demands the continued mobilisation of domestic resources to finance public goods and services.

Curtailing illicit financial flows (IFFs) and combatting tax evasion are therefore important elements in supporting South Africa's fiscal position and increasing the potential for revenue growth. Several recent studies have documented substantial IFF outflows during the last decade, from South Africa and the continent overall, reflecting South Africa's challenge in successfully combatting IFFs. The amounts of IFFs leaving the country during the last decade, for instance, are estimated to range from about USD 14 billion to USD 20 billion annually as reported by AU/ECA (2015[1]) and GFI (2021[2]) respectively. However, some have called into question these estimates, as they are often based on aggregated data, which may conflate measurement error in cross-border statistics with illicit activity. At the same time, better policies require more analysis to disentangle and analyse the different contributing IFF categories and assess existing policy measures that are being taken to tackle them.

In an effort to assess IFFs more precisely and to support domestic revenue mobilisation, the OECD and South Africa's National Treasury have embarked on a joint project to assess the IFFs landscape in South Africa. The project focuses on assessing the impact of recent tax compliance initiatives, understanding where continuing gaps remain, and estimating historical non-compliant foreign wealth and resulting illicit outflows. By analysing anonymised individual tax data on foreign income declarations, applications to Voluntary Disclosure Programmes (VDPs) and exchanged accounts under the Common Reporting Standard (CRS), the project not only attempts to provide an order of magnitude of IFFs from South Africa in recent years but also evaluates the behaviour of taxpayers facing increasing global and domestic tax transparency. The project uses tax data to measure all IFFs.

The analysis shows that tax evasion has a long history in South Africa and has been concentrated among the very wealthy and top income earners. It is estimated that in 2018, non-compliant assets worth between USD 40 billion and USD 54 billion were held in international financial centres (IFCs) based on cross-border financial account data from the CRS. Based on these figures and a number of assumptions, the analysis estimates that these deposits would suggest that annual IFFs of between USD 3.5 billion and USD 5 billion have left the country per year over the last decade. The analysis and the estimation process will be provided in more detail below. While this analysis is based on well-founded assumptions, it relies on new data of foreign financial accounts that has never before been used in the analysis of IFFs and allows for a more accurate understanding of IFFs than previous studies.

The analysis suggests that some progress has been made in supporting taxpayer compliance in recent years. Examining taxpayer data, revenue source data and data from VDPs shows evidence of increasing taxpayer compliance and additional revenues collected as a response to multilateral tax transparency initiatives that increase the global risk of detection, such as the CRS. Taxpayer responsiveness to domestic policy initiatives such as VDPs has also been triggered by the commencement of the automatic exchange of information (AEOI), successfully encouraging evaders to declare non-compliant foreign accounts. Taxpayer compliance, particularly among high-income earners, may be expected to further increase amid the rising risk of future detection.

Exchanged CRS information can provide new insights beyond other available data sources related to individual cross-border finance and can become an essential tool in the fight against tax evasion and IFFs, but additional work is required to get the most from the initiative. Successfully linking the foreign CRS accounts of South Africans with existing income tax returns is key to credibly increasing the risk of detection and the potential for revenue collection. The analysis suggests that matching CRS records to domestic tax records continues to be a challenge for South Africa. Accounts from IFCs did however have a higher match rate than non-IFCs. The number of matched taxpayers not having declared their foreign income is also found to be large, suggesting that exchanged CRS data provides an important new data source for tax authorities. Effective use of CRS data also depends on the capacity of tax administrations to exploit the information transmitted. Increasing the use of existing EOI treaties for requesting information held abroad on specific taxpayers, particularly with well-known IFCs, should be a key priority. Better domestic enforcement not only demands an enhancement of inter-agency collaboration across the different relevant authorities but also a strengthening of data processing capacity to enable a comprehensive analysis of taxpayer information. These improvements will not only result in much needed additional revenue gains but will also help to increase overall progressivity in the tax system.

The report is structured in six different chapters. Chapter 2 provides an overview of macroeconomic and fiscal developments in South Africa since the global financial crisis. A particular emphasis has been put on the recent economic scarring inflicted by the COVID-19 pandemic, with a particular focus on its impact on South Africa's near-term fiscal space. Chapter 3 discusses the concepts of IFFs, how they relate to the South African context and provides an overview of South Africa's participation in multilateral initiatives to combat tax evasion. Chapter 4 presents an overview of the structure and recent development in the South African tax system, stressing in particular the need for a well-functioning income tax system due to an increasing reliance on direct taxes. Commencing with the data-driven analysis, chapter 5 provides a quantitative analysis by assessing tax compliance over time amid a variety of tax transparency initiatives implemented in South Africa. It also evaluates the effectiveness of VDPs and looks into the income and wealth characteristics of applicants. Chapter 6 estimates the amount of previously 'hidden' or non-compliant foreign wealth and the size of IFFs in South Africa by relying on several different descriptive and quantitative approaches. Chapter 7 concludes the report.

References

AU/ECA (2015), *Track it! Stop it! Get it! Report of the High Level Panel of Illicit Financial Flows from Africa*, https://repository.uneca.org/bitstream/handle/10855/22695/b11524868.pdf?sequence=3&isAllowed=y. [1]

Global Financial Integrity (2021), *Trade-Related Illicit Financial Flows in 134 Developing Countries: 2009-2018*, https://secureservercdn.net/50.62.198.97/34n.8bd.myftpupload.com/wp-content/uploads/2021/12/IFFs-Report-2021.pdf?time=1643653304. [2]

2 Macroeconomic and fiscal context in South Africa

Key messages

- This chapter provides an overview of the macroeconomic and fiscal environment in South Africa, focusing in particular on the recent impact of the COVID-19 pandemic.
- During the last decade, South Africa's economic performance has been relatively poor, resulting in low growth and persistent socio-economic challenges such as high income and wealth inequality, low intergenerational mobility, and rising unemployment rates.
- COVID-19 has exacerbated these issues and comprehensive fiscal measures to cushion its impact, though helpful, have resulted in declining economic activity and an increasingly unsustainable debt trajectory.
- While not a 'silver bullet', combatting illicit financial flows has an important role to play in reinforcing South Africa's fiscal position and increasing its potential for revenue growth.

Macroeconomic environment

The decade following the global financial crisis has been characterised amongst emerging and developing economies by relatively robust average growth rates. Buoyed by an accommodative monetary policy environment, intensifying global trade and accompanying overall benign investor sentiment, emerging and developing economies managed to grow at high rates and outperformed OECD economies (Figure 2.1). While OECD countries expanded their economies on average by 2% annually before the COVID-19 pandemic, Sub-Saharan Africa achieved a growth rate of around 3.5%. China and India experienced economic growth of 7.7% and 6.7% respectively.

With an average growth rate of about 1.7% between 2010 and 2019, South Africa's economic performance has been relatively modest compared to other BRICS economies throughout the last decade. Growth rates trended downwards in the aftermath of the 2008/2009 recession in South Africa, with economic expansion weakening further in recent years, held back largely by structural country-specific factors. Supply side constraints in key network industries such as electricity – resulting in still regular power outages - telecommunications and transportation have played a major role in modest growth outcomes, combined with low levels of business confidence amid policy uncertainty (OECD, 2021[1]). As a result, real per capita income has also been falling since 2015 and is now back to its level in 2005 (World Bank, 2021[2]).

Figure 2.1. Annual GDP growth across different regions during 2010 - 20

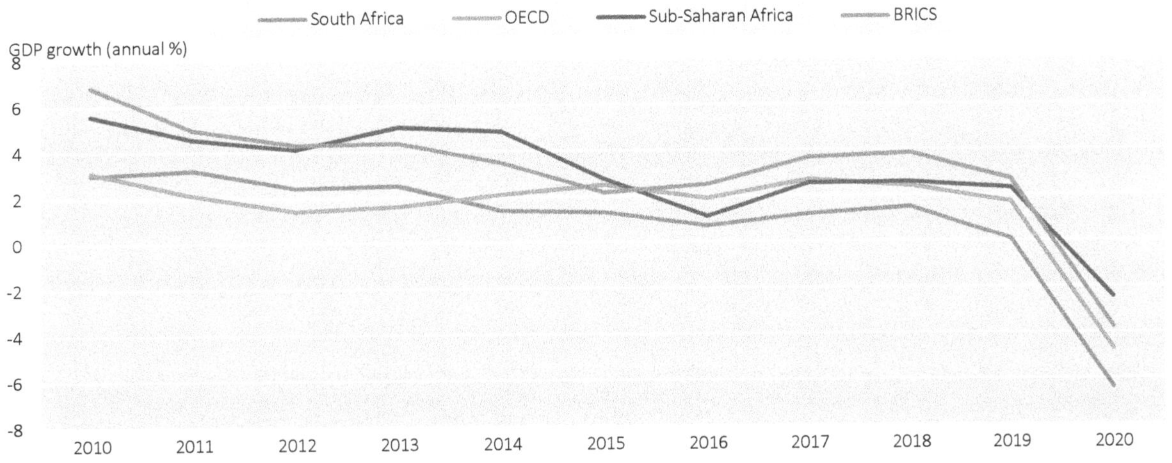

Note: Growth rates for the OECD, Sub-Saharan Africa and the BRICS (Brazil, Russia, India, China, South Africa) country groups are expressed as unweighted averages across all included economies.
Source: OECD Economic Outlook No 110 database and World Bank Development Indicators 2021.

StatLink ⏵ https://stat.link/jpagb5

South Africa's level of inequality is a challenge and progress in enhancing the wellbeing of its citizens has been slower relative to major improvements during the previous two decades. Structural inequality remains persistent due to a highly unequal distribution of income and wealth, as well as low intergenerational mobility. Income inequality, measured by the consumption expenditure Gini coefficient (0.65), decreased between 2006 and 2010. However, since then this decline has not continued despite increasing social transfers to over 3% of GDP, which has been higher than in many other developing countries or the OECD average (OECD, 2020[3]). Wealth inequality with a Gini coefficient of 0.9 is even higher (Orthofer, 2016[4]). The percentage of the population below the upper-middle-income-country poverty line (USD 5.50 per day per person) fell from 68% to 56% between 2005 and 2010 but has since trended slightly upwards to 57% in 2015 and was projected to reach 60% in 2020. Unemployment also remains high and has been growing from 22% in 2008 to 34% in the third quarter of 2021 after a steep decline of over 10% during the early 2000s. Currently the unemployment rate is highest among young people, at around 63% (World Bank, 2021[2]). Unmet needs in education, health and infrastructure and corruption have also been a policy challenge (Figure 2.2). These factors highlight the need to reduce income and wealth inequality in South Africa, including through the tax system.

Figure 2.2. Challenges in well-being and inequality

OECD Better Life Index, country rankings from 1 (best) to 40 (worst), 2018 or latest available

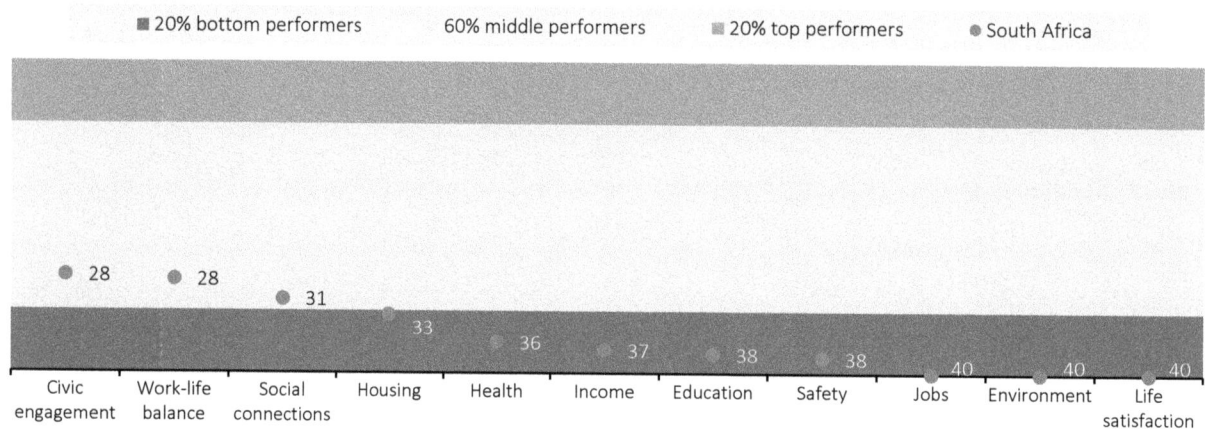

Note: Each well-being dimension is measured by one to four indicators from the OECD Better Life Index set for 37 OECD countries as well as Brazil, Russian Federation and South Africa. Normalised indicators are averaged with equal weights.
Source: OECD (2021), OECD Better Life Index, https://www.oecdbetterlifeindex.org.

StatLink https://stat.link/0rl8ij

While the economy's relatively rapid recovery after the global financial crisis was aided by expansionary fiscal policy and public investment, investment growth has declined since then. This has contributed to the lower economic growth in recent years in a context of also declining private investment (Figure 2.3). Investment has weakened, particularly in the manufacturing sector, reflecting a deterioration in solvency but also in the business climate more broadly, with exacerbating factors including rising political uncertainty and social risks (OECD, 2021[1]). Public investment in infrastructure by state-owned enterprises (SOEs) and the general government has been the dominant supporting factor for economic growth in recent years (National Treasury of South Africa, 2021[5]). Increasing public investment from 3.6% to 5% of GDP would boost potential growth if cost containment and planning as well as a better cost-benefit analysis are implemented (OECD, 2020[3]). This highlights the importance of domestic resource mobilisation to support such investments.

Figure 2.3. Contributions to investment growth on the decline

Contributions to investment growth by investor in % points

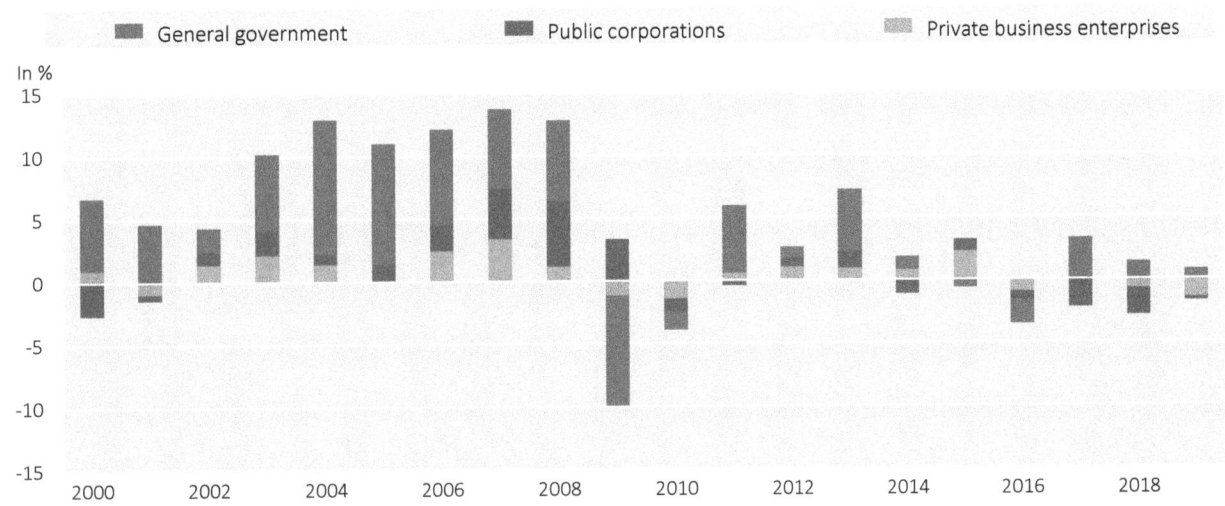

Source: South African Reserve Bank.

StatLink https://stat.link/w678nv

The challenging economic growth trajectory and decline in investment growth has been accompanied by a fall in overall productivity. While total factor productivity had accelerated to reach 3% in the 2000s, it has slowed sharply following the 2008/2009 recession and together with a contraction in employment, has triggered a decline in growth. The loss in productivity has particularly been concentrated in important, often state-owned, network industries such as the utilities, mining, construction, and telecommunications sectors (Hausmann et al., 2022[6]).

The post-global financial crisis period has been marked by sustained capital flows to South Africa, with some risks due to potential volatility. Capital inflows have supported economic growth and supplemented to some extent the decline in domestic investment. In recent years, however, South Africa has become more reliant on relatively large but volatile portfolio investment flows, despite foreign investors having reduced their investment in the economy on net (Figure 2.4). A similar story also applies to direct investment, albeit to a lower extent. In terms of bilateral partners, the United Kingdom and the Netherlands account for over half of FDI liabilities (stocks). The United States account for approximately half of portfolio investment liabilities (stocks).

Over the past two decades, South Africa has gradually increased its investment outflows, largely explained by the loosening of exchange controls. Net FDI outflows have been largely positive but on a downward trend since 2014 and entered negative territory during the recent pandemic. The largest FDI assets have consistently been liabilities of China, South Africa's largest export destination. Major destinations are also the United Kingdom, the United States and the European Union, but also smaller international financial centres (IFCs) such as Jersey, Mauritius or Switzerland. While less in overall size but still substantial, portfolio investments and to a lesser extent bank assets have also been invested in the United Kingdom and the United States but also in IFCs such as the Isle of Man, Luxembourg and Guernsey.

Figure 2.4. FDI and portfolio flows in South Africa

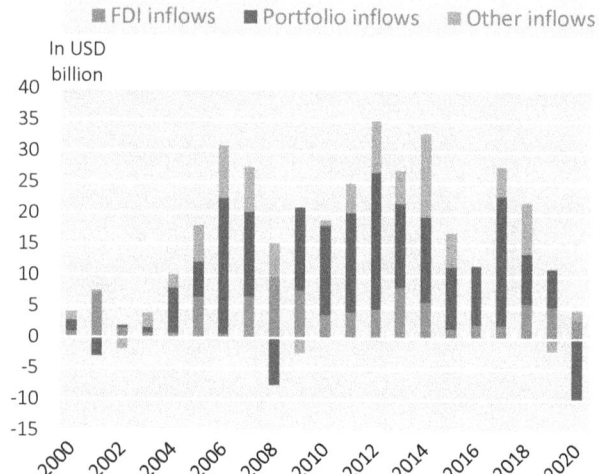

Panel A: Net capital inflows

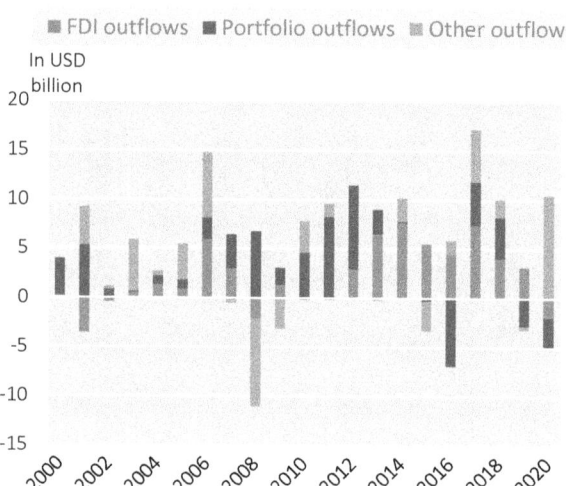

Panel B: Net capital outflows

Source: IMF Balance of Payments Statistics.

StatLink ⟶ https://stat.link/847yk2

As a result, the net international investment position has turned positive in 2015, primarily due to changes in the valuation of South Africa's currency. South Africa's position is expected to moderate further in the medium term due to consistently large current account deficits, though these have reversed since the COVID-19 crisis. While the asset position has been largely fuelled by direct investments, the liabilities side consists to a large extent of portfolio investments (around 50% during the last decade). Due to South Africa's deep capital markets, implying a low reliance of domestic banks on foreign capital funding and prudential limits to foreign exchange liabilities of banks, foreign portfolio investments flow into domestic equity and bonds. This means that foreign investors rather than domestic borrowers absorb the currency risk associated with these investments and react to changes in economic fundamentals, business sentiment and policy uncertainty. As South Africa's liabilities are mostly denominated in local currency and its international assets in foreign currency, any shock to the economy which causes exchange rate depreciation will also tend to improve the level of the net international investment position and vice versa (Benetrix et al., 2019[7]).

Capital account liberalisation

Recently South Africa has started the process of further liberalising its capital account following the country's request to adhere to the OECD's Code of Liberalisation of Capital Movements (CLCM) in October 2017. This entails the replacement of the existing exchange control regulation with a new capital flow management system. The present system, which has been in place since 1995 and gradually adapted to the increasing global integration of South Africa's economy, allowed the country to attract important inward capital flows supporting domestic investment. Some scholars have argued that restrictions on outward investments were aimed at protecting the limited domestic savings and prohibiting undesired capital outflows (Farrell and Todani, 2006[8]). Non-residents thus could invest freely in domestic capital and money markets and were able to buy and sell securities and instruments. In contrast, investments abroad by residents and domestic companies had been largely restricted and required prior authorisation from the Reserve Bank and National Treasury. The exchange regulation system, however, has suffered from several issues such as a lack of monitoring of financial outflows by non-residents or outflows to the other Common Monetary Area countries, which, despite having substantially implemented similar exchange control systems, their financial and regulatory systems may not reflect the same level of sophistication (Wang et al., 2007[9]).[1]

The regulatory shift to the capital flow management system can assist in South Africa's efforts to combat IFFs by realigning resources and improving capital flow management. This approach is aligned with the multilateral CLCM and consists primarily of a fundamental change in the legislative perspective applied to capital flows. While South African legislation so far operates under a 'positive list' approach, where cross-border capital movements are subject to approval or not permitted unless stated otherwise, the CLCM applies a 'negative list' approach where everything is permitted unless otherwise stated (OECD, 2021[10]). By relying on a transparent, risk-based approval framework, the new capital flow management system aims to more thoroughly monitor cross-border capital flows and prudentially regulate foreign exposure of banks and institutional investors according to global best practices. Moreover, reinforcing co-operation between relevant authorities is expected to further mitigate risks to the country's tax and investment base such as base erosion and profit shifting, illicit financial flows (IFFs) and tax evasion. This approach should also further foster South Africa's attractiveness as an investment destination and a financial hub more generally.

Fiscal environment

When the global financial crisis hit in 2008/09, South Africa had been running small budget surpluses. The debt-to-GDP ratio was under 30% (Figure 2.5). This allowed for increased government spending, part of which was initially justified as countercyclical stimulus, but which was not subsequently reversed. Persistent fiscal deficits have since caused a strong increase in the debt-to-GDP ratio. Some attempts at fiscal consolidation have been made over the last decade. These were supported primarily by tax increases, while aggregate spending kept growing or failed to decline as a share of GDP. The main drivers of these spending increases were above-inflation growth in the public sector wage bill, rising debt-service costs, and liquidity support for SOEs (OECD, 2020[3]). The fiscal position was thus already challenging prior to the COVID-19 pandemic, with the fiscal deficit in 2019 standing at 4.9% of GDP and the debt-to-GDP ratio at 56.3%.

Figure 2.5. Debt and debt-service costs in South Africa

Development of government gross debt and debt-service costs in % of GDP

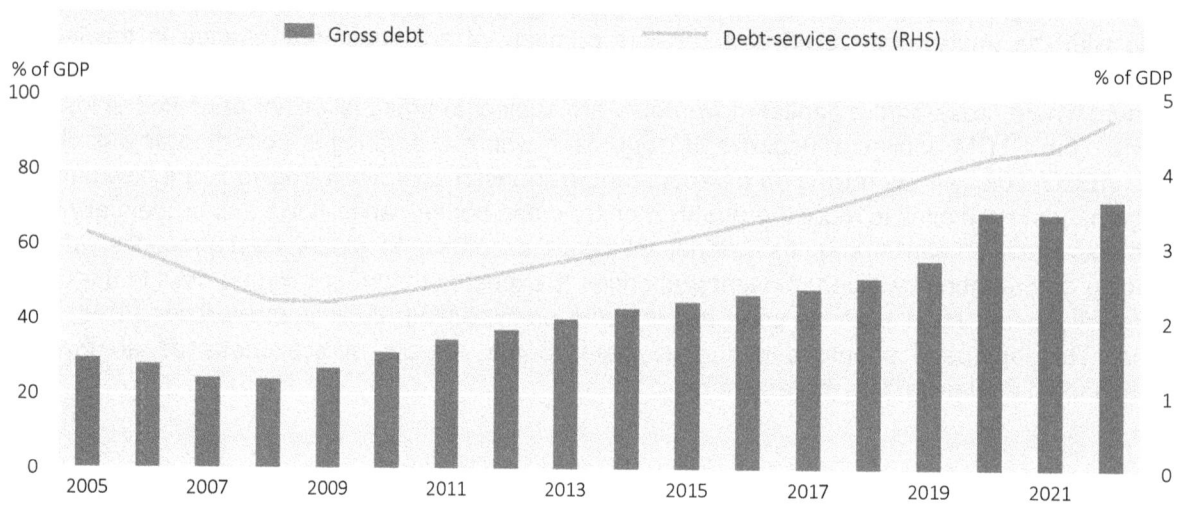

Source: National Treasury and IMF Fiscal Monitor.

StatLink https://stat.link/cavflj

South Africa belonged to the top 10 global economies in terms of outstanding external debt by the end of 2019. Its external debt stock rose by 9% during 2018-2019, largely driven through its USD 5 billion sovereign issuance, its largest ever issued international bond. This bond alone accounted for 25% of all bond issuance in Sub-Saharan Africa (World Bank, 2021[11]). Largely resulting from its well-developed domestic capital market, South Africa has about 90% of its public debt denominated in its domestic currency, while 10% is held in foreign currency. The continuing depreciation of the Rand since the global financial crisis has thus had a more limited effect on the value of outstanding foreign debt. However, a large proportion of this debt is held by foreigners (South African Reserve Bank, 2021[12]). South Africa lost its investment-grade credit rating from all major rating agencies in March 2020, raising debt service costs even higher. As of April 2020, Standard & Poor's has lowered the rating further into non-investment grade. However, recent efforts to switch out of shorter-term bonds into longer-dated debt have prolonged the maturity profile and should allow South Africa to better manage refinancing risks.[2]

National Treasury projections of South Africa's debt-to-GDP trajectory for the medium term expect a continuation of this challenging fiscal environment. Despite scenario updates, in light of the already challenging environment before the pandemic, implemented policy initiatives to support the economy and resulting contractions in GDP due to protracted lockdowns have put further upward pressure on the debt ratio (National Treasury of South Africa, 2021[5]). Due to recent windfall revenues from the commodity sector, however, the most recent revision of the forecast projects debt reaching stabilisation in 2024/2025 at a level of 75% of GDP (Figure 2.6). This outlook, however, remains contingent on the envisaged restraints in expenditure growth and supporting measures to raise economic growth.

Figure 2.6. Debt trajectories in South Africa

A comparison of debt-to-GDP trajectories relative to the underlying policy implementation and growth projections

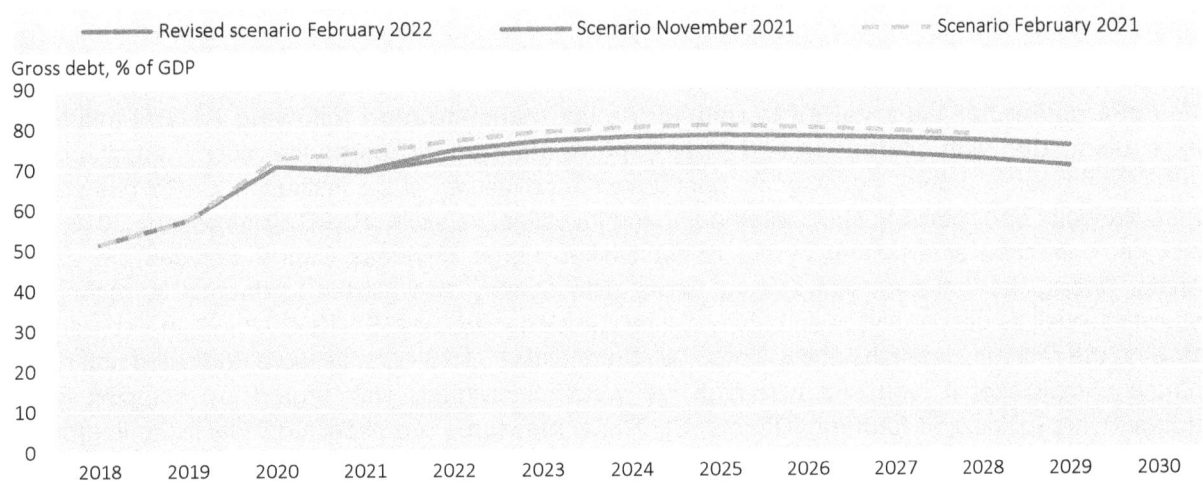

Note: The different debt trajectories represent scenarios from the budget reports presented by the National Treasury before the parliament in February 2021, November 2021, and February 2022.
Source: National Treasury.

StatLink https://stat.link/ulh71b

South Africa's tax-to-GDP ratio has been constantly well above comparable developing and middle-income economies but lower than the OECD average. In 2018, South Africa's tax-to-GDP ratio stood at 24%, which is lower than the OECD average of 34%, but considerably higher than other African countries or the average of large emerging economies such as in Brazil, China, India or South Africa (BRICS) (Figure 2.7). During the period of 2009 to 2018, the ratio increased from 21% to 24% of South African GDP, exceeding the growth rates in the BRICS, other African countries and also the OECD, moving South Africa closer to the tax-to-GDP levels of advanced economies. South Africa's tax system is discussed in more detail in Chapter 4.

Figure 2.7. Tax-to-GDP ratios in selected regions, 2009 to 2018

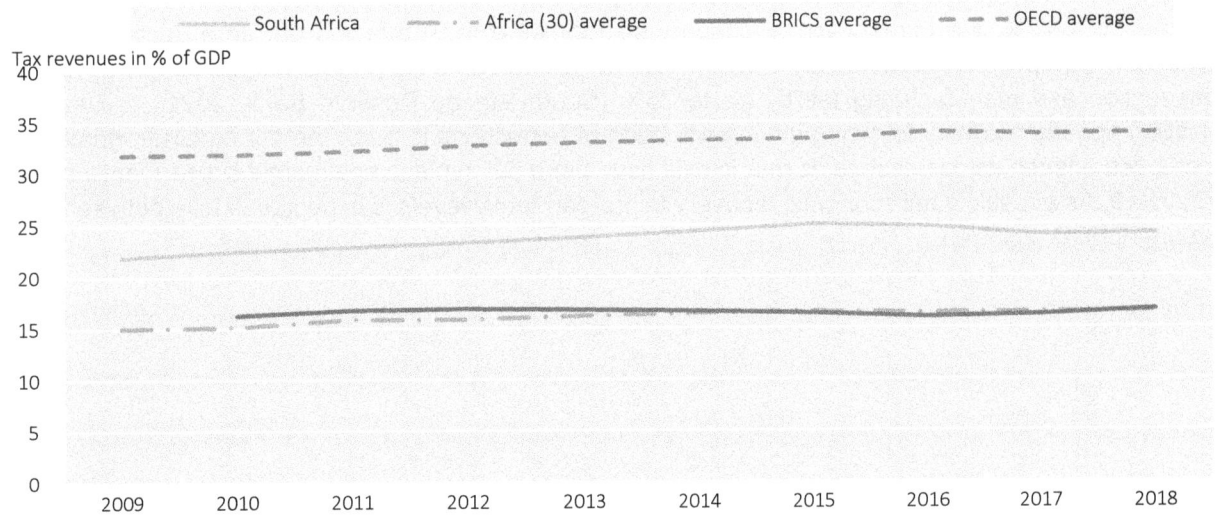

Source: Authors' calculations based on OECD Tax Statistics (database) and World Bank, 2021.

StatLink https://stat.link/fsxk3a

In light of increasing spending needs, the government announced several tax policy changes in the 2022 budget for both firms and households. In an effort to simultaneously alleviate the tax burden for companies and broaden the income tax base, the corporate income tax rate will be lowered from 28% to 27% as of 1 April 2022. This will be accompanied by a limitation in interest deductions and assessed losses. The personal income tax brackets and rebates will be increased by 4.5%, in line with the inflation rate.

The government has also started to rebuild the tax administration following several challenging years associated with corruption and state capture charges. Following the recommendations of the SARS Commission, a body inquiring into past governance failures at the institution, SARS has started to renew its focus by expanding specialised audit and investigative skills (SARS Commission, 2018[13]). For instance, enhanced assessment by the re-established Large Business Centre includes the abuse of transfer pricing, tax base erosion and tax crime. The agency also started to deepen its technological capacity as well as data analytics and artificial intelligence capabilities (SARS, 2020[14]). In February 2020, following the recommendations of the Davis Tax Committee, SARS established a dedicated unit to better enforce compliance of high and ultra-high net wealth individuals with regards to complex financial arrangements (discussed further in Chapter 3). These measures are expected to facilitate improved tax collection and enhanced tax compliance. To fund increased responsibilities and technological implementation, additional spending of ZAR 3 billion has been allocated to SARS (National Treasury of South Africa, 2021[5]). These efforts to strengthen the tax administration come amid increasing public debate around the importance of successfully tackling illicit financial flows (IFFs) in their various forms and strengthening domestic resource mobilisation, as will be discussed below.

Impact of COVID-19

The COVID-19 pandemic has worsened the economic and fiscal outlook in South Africa. Due to the rapid spread of the virus as of early 2020 and the subsequent stringent lockdown introduced at the end of March, South Africa's economy suffered a sharp contraction in the second quarter of 2020. Relative to the fourth quarter of 2019, GDP contracted by just over 16% during the first and the second quarter, dwarfing the impact of the global financial crisis and any other contraction period in South African historical data.[3] The economic contraction has also been more severe compared to the OECD or the average of emerging market economies (Figure 2.8). Nearly all industries experienced a significant drop in activity in the second quarter. While service and finance industries showed some resilience and suffered an average reduction in growth of 30.7%, the primary and secondary sectors were most affected due to a decline in global demand, a disruption of global supply chains, and a drop in commodity prices. Output in mining, tourism, construction and manufacturing fell by up to 75% (South African Reserve Bank, 2021[12]). Despite a relatively speedy recovery following the interim lifting of restrictions through the third quarter, growth has since been uneven across sectors as restrictions have been put in place again amid subsequent waves of COVID-19. As a result, a full economic recovery to pre-pandemic levels is expected to take between 3 and 5 years (OECD, 2021[15]).

Figure 2.8. COVID-19 and economic growth impact

Real GDP trajectories during the COVID-19 pandemic

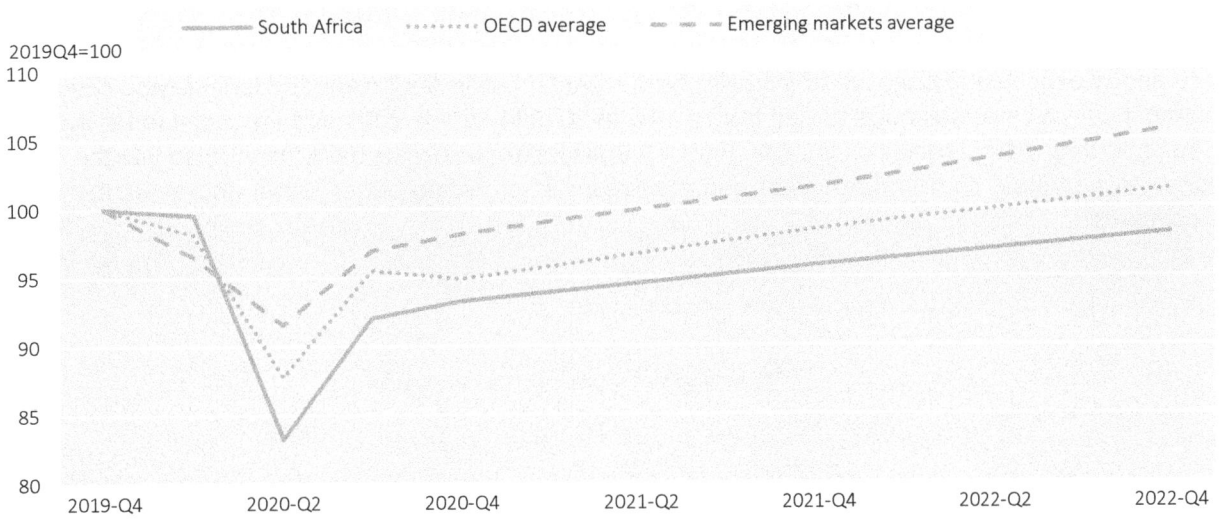

Note: Real GDP trajectories are based on the OECD's December 2020 projections and displayed relative to the base quarter 2019Q4. Emerging markets average refers to the average of major non-OECD economies from Latin America, Eastern Europe and Asia.
Source: OECD Economic Outlook Database.

StatLink https://stat.link/b65r0t

In an attempt to alleviate its impact, South Africa responded to the pandemic with a series of decisive fiscal policy measures. The government remained committed to supporting firms and households despite limited fiscal space. All available social grants were augmented and new schemes were implemented to provide support to workers including those in the informal sector. Specific schemes were activated targeting businesses in the hardest-hit sectors such as tourism. Programmes such as the COVID-19 loan guarantee scheme, initially implemented in early 2021 (ZAR 18.1 billion or 0.4% of GDP guaranteed by the end of March), were extended until June 2021. Eligibility to the COVID-19 social relief of distress grants for low-income households and the temporary employment relief scheme have been extended to up to six months, both programmes ending in March 2023. Funding for the public employment initiative and for provincial hospitals was increased by ZAR 11 billion (0.2% of GDP) in 2021/22. Up to ZAR 10.3 billion had been provided for the vaccination rollout over the next two years, adding potentially ZAR 7 billion in supplementary contingency funding given uncertain vaccination campaign expenses.

Emergency provision of liquidity has further been accompanied by tax measures to temporarily reduce the tax burden for companies and citizens. The tax policies implemented on an immediate basis range from tax deferrals and more flexible tax debt repayment or tax refunds to tax rate cuts (OECD, 2021[16]). South Africa allowed large businesses to apply directly to the tax administration to defer tax payments without incurring penalties if they could prove that they were unable to pay their tax liability as a result of the COVID-19 crisis. There were temporary increases to tax deductions for charitable donations. Changes to the corporate tax base to provide liquidity support included the following measures: South Africa postponed the decision to limit net interest expense deductions to 30% of taxable income and to limit the use of assessed losses carried forward to at least January 2022. Companies could also profit from accelerated tax refunds. Moreover, households were granted an increase in the annual contribution limit to tax free savings accounts by ZAR 3 000 from 1 March 2020 to increase savings. Overall the government mobilised over 10% of GDP (around ZAR 500 billion, with ZAR 200 billion as contingent liability) for new spending, reprioritisation, tax relief and loan guarantees. Despite the implementation of these supportive policy measures, the impact of the pandemic on the tax base has nonetheless led to significantly diminished tax revenues and the largest tax shortfall on record (National Treasury of South Africa, 2021[5]).

The implementation of emergency tax measures and the accompanying shortfall in tax revenues has resulted in further challenges for South Africa's debt situation. Debt sustainability has significantly deteriorated as the debt-to-GDP ratio grew from about 53% in early 2019 to over 70% in late 2020 and is expected to continue to increase further. Amid falling tax revenues, debt-service costs as a share of total tax revenues have surged from a 14% in 2019 to 19% in 2021 and are projected to increase further following a slight reduction in 2022 (Figure 2.9). Debt-service costs have thus turned into the fastest growing expenditure item in the budget and may result in crowding-out of social and economic public investments.

Figure 2.9. COVID-19 and South Africa's fiscal picture

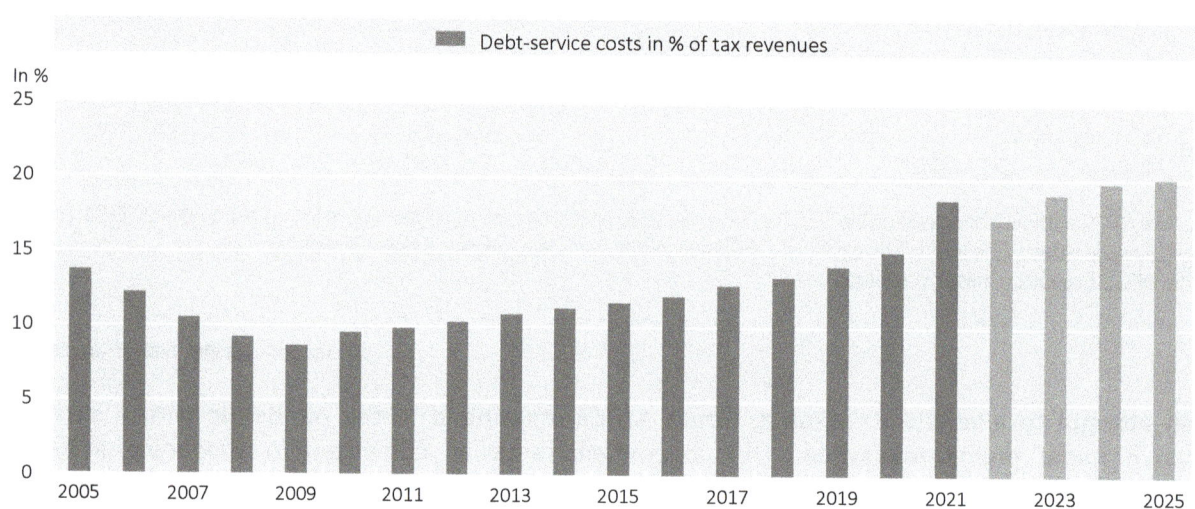

Note: Years are fiscal years. The light-grey bars show medium-term estimates from the Budget Review 2022.
Source: National Treasury.

StatLink ⟶ https://stat.link/ipk2tj

In addition, South Africa's response to the economic challenges arising from the pandemic involved an aggressive easing in monetary policy. Between July 2019 and July 2020, SARB gradually lowered the repurchase ("repo") rate, the policy rate of the central bank, from 6.75% to 3.5%, an easing of 325 basis points. The strong monetary policy response to the pandemic was shaped primarily by the clear disinflation that started in 2017 and by 2020 had opened up policy space. The repo rate was kept constant for most of 2020 and 2021 to alleviate the contraction and support the recovery (Loewald, 2021[17]). However, due to rising inflation, SARB has started to raise the repo rate with two consecutive 25 basis point increases reaching 4% with further gradual increases expected to follow. In addition, the Reserve Bank increased its interventions in the money market to provide more liquidity to financial institutions and ease lending conditions. SARB has also initiated a program to buy government bonds in the market, ensuring the liquidity of the debt market.

Despite the strong policy response, the pandemic hit South Africa's labour market hard, creating strong cyclical underemployment. Largely a result of containment measures during the first two quarters in 2020, the employment rate fell by about 6%. As people dropped out of the labour force, the participation rate declined by 13% (Figure 2.10, Panel A). Moreover, people temporarily stopped looking for work, which caused the unemployment rate to fall temporarily amid an increasing trend (Figure 2.10., Panel B).

Although the labour market showed signs of recovery from the third quarter of 2020 onwards, largely driven by the public sector, both the employment and the participation rate remained significantly below their pre-crisis levels. Also unemployment bounced back to an even slightly higher rate than before the crisis-induced drop. The flattening of all curves after the interim recovery points to potentially protracted negative effects of the pandemic for the quarters to come. This lack of labour market resilience, however, is not unique to the current pandemic (Duval, Ji and Shibata, 2021[18]). Unemployment in South Africa is more responsive to business cycle movements than in other emerging and advanced economies, partly reflecting inflexible labour market institutions, relatively low prevalence of informality and high cyclicality of youth unemployment.

Figure 2.10. The impact of COVID-19 on the labour market

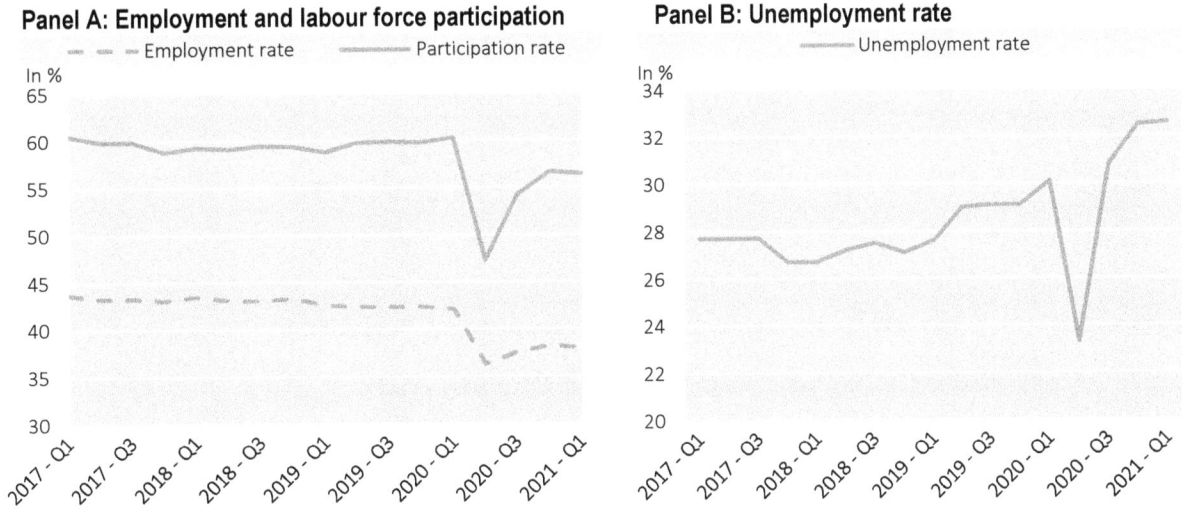

Note: All indicators refer to percentage shares of the population aged between 15 and 64.
Source: Quarterly Labour Force Survey (Q1 2017 – Q1 2021), Statistics South Africa.

StatLink ⇨ https://stat.link/mod675

The pandemic also had a significant impact on capital flows to the African continent and South Africa in particular. FDI flows to Africa declined from USD 47 billion in 2019 by 16% in 2020 to USD 40 billion – a level last seen 15 years ago. FDI inflows to South Africa declined by 39% in 2020 on a year-on-year basis, facing the largest slump by an individual country on the continent during the early phase of the pandemic. Cross-border mergers and acquisitions, although forming a relatively small part of total inflows, took the largest hit and dropped by 52% (UNCTAD, 2021[19]).

The COVID-19 crisis further illustrated the dynamics at work during sudden stops of more volatile portfolio flows. Compared to the global financial crisis, similar factors have been identified as the main triggers for the sharp reversal in non-resident capital flows to emerging economies. The sudden outflow in February 2020 had largely been triggered by a sudden shift in investors' risk appetite towards safe-haven assets as well as country-specific factors such as a decline in economic activity, also putting pressure on the currency (Figure 2.11) (de Crescenzio and Lepers, 2021[20]). Scale and speed, however, have been about four times larger than during the global financial crisis. South Africa, as a commodity exporter, was also hit by a second, parallel exogenous shock when commodity prices fell sharply (though these have risen recently). As a result, non-resident capital flows into South African assets switched from a net inflow of about USD 10.6 billion in 2019 to a net outflow of about USD 6.6 billion in 2020 (South African Reserve Bank, 2021[12]). Later in 2020, when capital flows again picked up substantially across many emerging market economies, domestic pull factors such as the decisive macroeconomic policies to alleviate the crisis impact played an important role. However, given the outlook of a relatively slow economic recovery, a full recovery in investment flows may lag behind other large emerging economies.

Figure 2.11. The onset of COVID-19 resulted in pronounced reversal of capital flows

Portfolio inflows by month, January 2019 – October 2021

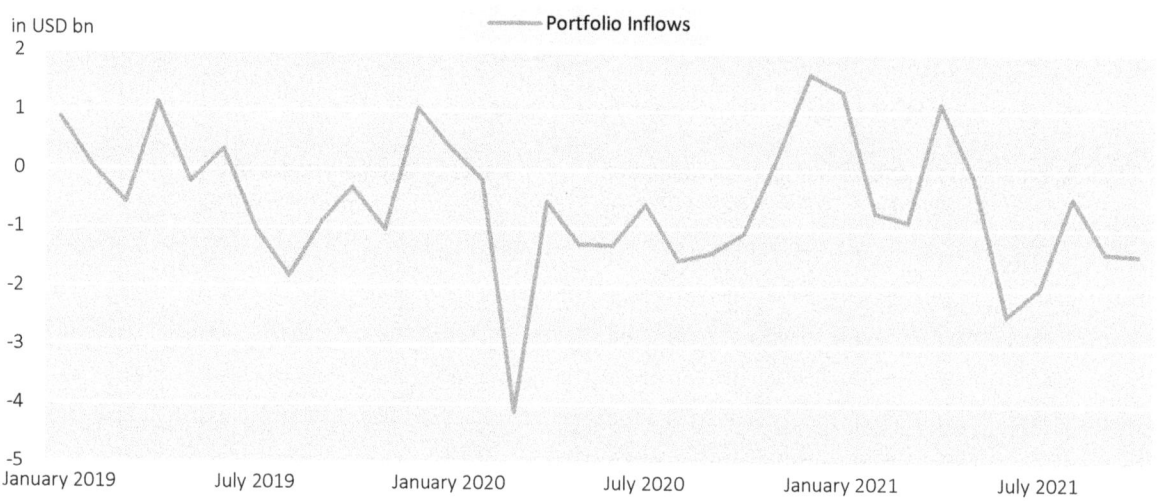

Source: De Crescenzio and Lepers (2021[20]) based on data from the South African Reserve Bank.

StatLink https://stat.link/n4xr2z

Conclusion

Like in many other advanced and emerging countries, the pandemic has brought South Africa's economic and structural challenges to the forefront. South Africa's difficult situation of subdued growth, rising debt levels, socio-economic challenges of high inequality, poverty and unemployment rates leaves the country with limited fiscal space. While the situation was already challenging prior to the pandemic, COVID-19 has exacerbated these issues and the risks to a speedy recovery and the medium-term economic growth outlook have become more pronounced.

Fiscal support by the government has been rapid and comprehensive to alleviate the effects of the pandemic. However, while additional measures have been designed to underpin the economic recovery, they may further jeopardise debt sustainability and raise debt-service costs. Existing socio-economic challenges are likely to remain and may turn worse as past pandemics have been shown to often widen inequality further and may have ripple effects on poverty (Furceri et al., 2020[21]).

Curtailing IFFs and combatting tax evasion are thus important to reinforce South Africa's fiscal position and increase its potential for revenue growth. The need to return to a sustainable fiscal path amid spending pressures to alleviate ad hoc pandemic and long-term structural challenges will demand continued financial efforts from the government. Moreover, achieving the SDGs will require mobilising additional funding, in particular domestic resources, to finance public goods and services. While liberalising the capital account may attract important investment flows, more work is needed to ensure IFFs can be kept in check by capable and well-funded tax and financial authorities. This will help broaden the tax base and strengthen domestic resource mobilisation to raise much needed tax revenues and build greater confidence in public administration.

References

Benetrix, A. et al. (2019), *Cross-Border Currency Exposures*, International Monetary Fund, https://www.imf.org/-/media/Files/Publications/WP/2019/wpiea2019299-print-pdf.ashx. [7]

de Crescenzio, A. and E. Lepers (2021), "Extreme capital flow episodes from the Global Financial Crisis to COVID-19: An exploration with monthly data", *OECD Working Papers on International Investment*, No. 2021/05, OECD Publishing, Paris, https://dx.doi.org/10.1787/d557b9c4-en. [20]

Duval, R., Y. Ji and I. Shibata (2021), *Labor Market Reform Options to Boost Employment in South Africa*. [18]

English, B., K. Forbes and A. Ubide (eds.) (2021), *Weathering Covid: South Africa's central bank policy in 2020 and 2021*, CEPR Press, https://voxeu.org/system/files/epublication/Central%20banking%20in%20the%20covid%20era.pdf. [17]

Farrell, G. and K. Todani (2006), "Capital flows, capital control regulations and foreign exchange policies in South Africa", *South African Journal of Economic History*, Vol. 21/1-2, pp. 84-123, https://doi.org/Capital flows, capital control regulations and. [8]

Furceri, D. et al. (2020), "Will Covid-19 affect inequality? Evidence from past pandemics", *Covid Economics*, Vol. 12, pp. 138-157, https://cepr.org/file/9050/download?token=R4U7P5E8. [21]

Hausmann, R. et al. (2022), *Macroeconomic risk after a decade of microeconomic turbulence - South Africa 2007-2020*, https://growthlab.cid.harvard.edu/files/growthlab/files/2022-01-cid-wp-404-v2-macroeconomic-risks-south-africa.pdf. [6]

National Treasury of South Africa (2021), *Budget Review 2021*, http://www.treasury.gov.za/documents/National%20Budget/2021/review/FullBR.pdf. [5]

National Treasury of South Africa (2020), *Budget Review 2020*, http://www.treasury.gov.za/documents/national%20budget/2020/review/FullBR.pdf. [22]

OECD (2021), *COUNTRY TAX MEASURES IN RESPONSE TO COVID-19 PANDEMIC*, https://www.oecd.org/tax/covid-19-tax-policy-and-other-measures.xlsm (accessed on 7 September 2021). [16]

OECD (2021), *Economic Policy Reforms 2021: Going for Growth: Shaping a Vibrant Recovery*, OECD Publishing, Paris, https://dx.doi.org/10.1787/3c796721-en. [1]

OECD (2021), *OECD Code of Liberalisation of Capital Movements*, OECD Publishing, http://www.oecd.org/investment/codes.htm. [10]

OECD (2021), *OECD Economic Outlook*, OECD Publishing, Paris, https://dx.doi.org/10.1787/16097408. [15]

OECD (2020), *OECD Economic Surveys: South Africa*, OECD Publishing, Paris, https://dx.doi.org/10.1787/2218614x. [3]

Orthofer, A. (2016), "Wealth inequality in South Africa: Evidence from survey and tax data", *REDI3x3 Working Paper 15*, http://redi3x3.org/sites/default/files/Orthofer%202016%20REDI3x3%20Working%20Paper%2015%20-%20Wealth%20inequality.pdf. [4]

SARS (2020), *Strategic Plan: South African Revenue Service, 2020/21 - 2024/25*, https://www.sars.gov.za/wp-content/uploads/Enterprise/Strat/SARS-Strat-24-SARS-Strategic-Plan-2020-2021-2024-2025-11-May-2020.pdf. [14]

SARS Commission (2018), *Commission of Inquiry into Tax Administration and Governance by SARS - Final Report*, http://www.thepresidency.gov.za/download/file/fid/1462. [13]

South African Reserve Bank (2021), *Quarterly Bulletin March 2021*, https://www.resbank.co.za/content/dam/sarb/publications/quarterly-bulletins/quarterly-bulletin-publications/2021/march-2021/01Full%20Quarterly%20Bulletin%20March%202021.pdf. [12]

UNCTAD (2021), *World Investment Report 2021*, United Nations Publications, https://unctad.org/system/files/official-document/wir2021_en.pdf. [19]

Wang, J. et al. (2007), *The Common Monetary Area in Southern Africa: Shocks, Adjustment and Policy Challenges*, https://www.imf.org/external/pubs/ft/wp/2007/wp07158.pdf. [9]

World Bank (2021), *International Debt Statistics 2021*, https://openknowledge.worldbank.org/bitstream/handle/10986/34588/9781464816109.pdf. [11]

World Bank (2021), *South Africa Economic Update, Edition 13 : Building Back Better from COVID-19 with a Special Focus on Jobs*, World Bank, https://openknowledge.worldbank.org/handle/10986/35987. [2]

Notes

[1] The countries comprising the Common Monetary Area are Eswatini, Lesotho, Namibia and South Africa.

[2] According to National Treasury of South Africa (2020[22]), government bonds worth ZAR 247 billion have been switched into longer-term debt since 2015.

[3] Data available online at the South African Reserve Bank, historical macroeconomic time series information since 1960, gross domestic product at market prices (KBP6006D).

3 IFFs in the global and South African context

Key messages

- This chapter provides an overview of the global discussion of IFFs and provides orientation for defining IFFs in the present analysis.
- IFFs are harmful to developing countries as they effectively constitute tax revenues forgone that may have otherwise been spent on fostering socio-economic development.
- IFFs are inherently secret in nature and, therefore, are difficult to analyse, quantify and address.
- To date, no formal and commonly agreed definition of IFFs exists, which often results in a blurred line between 'illicit' but formally legal and illegal activities.
- For the purpose of this report, IFFs are defined as cross-border financial flows that are illegal either in their origin, transfer or use. This definition excludes tax avoidance, for example.
- Exchange of information is expected to play a key role in the detection of non-compliance in relation to cross-border transactions and assets held offshore.

Introduction

IFFs, and policies to combat them, represent a complex policy area. Due to their inherently secret nature, IFFs are difficult to analyse, quantify, and address. This chapter first provides a short synopsis of recent analysis of IFFs. It discusses how IFFs and their relevant subcomponents should be categorised. This is followed by a general overview of current global IFF estimates, a description of IFFs' harmfulness for developing countries, and measurement challenges. The chapter then focuses on the South African context. It discusses some of the country's still prevailing risks for IFFs, presents related estimates from the literature as well as important policy steps which have recently been implemented by South African authorities to rein in IFF leakages.

Defining IFFs

Defining IFFs is a challenging task. In the past two decades several attempts by international institutions and global policy actors to establish a widely acceptable definition have been made. Despite the emergence of certain commonalities in the various definitions, however, there remains no universally accepted definition. As a result, different terms in the area of IFFs have often been used interchangeably, obscuring the nuances relevant to designing appropriate policy responses or even successfully analysing and measuring IFFs. Only relatively recent definitions, for instance, departed from combining capital flight, the movement of funds abroad for better returns, with IFFs as revenue or proceeds derived from corruption, commercial activities or crime (Baker, 2005[1]). Based on this distinction, UNECA (2013[2]) referred to IFFs in its broadest sense as "money illegally earned, transferred or used".

Since then consensus about the cross-border nature of IFFs has emerged. The flows are generated by transactions, thereby contravening national or international laws. While, for instance, the World Bank has adopted the relatively broad notion of IFFs as money illegally earned, transferred or used, the cross-border element has strongly been emphasised. IFFs have been defined as cross-border movement of capital that is associated with illegal activity in the local jurisdiction (World Bank, 2017[3]). However, despite the term 'earned, transferred or used' being commonly used in the context of IFFs, the term "illicit financial flows" is still the subject of disagreement for statistical purposes. Without a consistent and commonly agreed upon definition, sound and comprehensive measurement as well as international comparison of IFFs will remain a challenge.

The 2030 Agenda for Sustainable Development of the United Nations identifies the reduction of IFFs as a key target for the Sustainable Development Goals (SDGs). In an effort to create an indicator to measure progress towards achieving this SDG target[1], UNCTAD and UNODC, in collaboration with national statistical offices, most recently established a Conceptual Framework for the Statistical Definition and the Measurement of IFFs (the framework) (UNODC/UNCTAD, 2020[4]). While the final SDG indicator envisions the measurement of the total value of IFFs, the framework seeks to establish a finer typology of IFFs and decomposes the aggregate category into a set of subcomponents to increase its applicability for statistical measurement and policy guidance. The resulting statistical definition considers IFFs as "financial flows that are illicit in origin, transfer or use, that reflect an exchange of value and that cross country borders". However, while three potentially overlapping forms of IFFs are specified in the above definition (origin, transfer and use), they are mapped on to two alternative types of IFFs. Specifically, UNODC/UNCTAD suggest that IFFs can be generated at two fundamental stages, namely during income generation and income management (though presumably IFFs could be generated if income is spent illegally as well). In the framework, IFFs can be linked to cross-border transactions in the context of producing illicit goods or services or directly generating illicit flows, but also to the use of illicit income for investment or consumption or illicit management of income generated from legal economic activity.

The recently proposed framework by UNODC and UNCTAD offers a further IFF typology. The framework therefore suggest that there are four main categories of activities that may generate IFFs: i) illicit tax and commercial activities, ii) illegal markets, iii) corruption, and iv) exploitation or theft-type activities and financing of terrorism and crime. These four main categories are shown in Figure 3.1.

Figure 3.1. UN Categorisation of IFFs

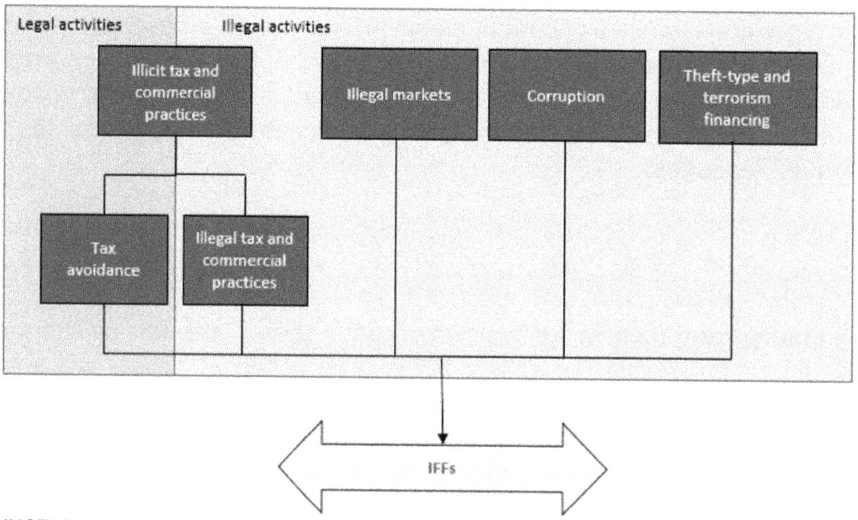

Source: UNODC and UNCTAD.

Most of these IFF categories can be related to clearly-defined crimes with associated financial flows crossing borders. IFFs from illegal markets involve criminal activities where income is generated through the exchange or trade of illegal goods or services. They include any type of trafficking in goods, such as drugs and firearms, or services, such as smuggling of migrants. IFFs from corruption include bribery, embezzlement, abuse of functions, trading in influence or illicit enrichment. Again, where the associated flows cross borders these would be IFFs. Similarly, financial flows related to exploitation-type activities such as slavery or trafficking in persons as well as financing of crime and terrorism that cross borders fall under the IFF definition as well. Proceeds from all of these activities are considered IFFs when they lead, directly or indirectly, to cross-border flows or when financial assets are transferred to commit crimes or have their origin in the above crimes (UNODC/UNCTAD, 2020[4]).

The difference between IFFs and tax avoidance

In the UNODC/UNCTAD framework illicit tax and commercial IFFs emerge as a category subdivided into illegal and legal activities. The illegal component of this category refers to illicit practices by legal entities or individuals with the aim to conceal revenues or reduce tax liabilities. Resulting IFFs include practices such as tariff, duty and revenue offences, tax evasion, contravention of exchange controls, competition offences and market manipulation amongst others, most of them unobserved.

The key form of IFF generated legally in the UNODC/UNCTAD framework is tax avoidance. Tax avoidance, while legal by definition, can also drain domestic resources and reduce government revenues. Given that these effects are negative and in some ways similar to the effects resulting from illegal IFFs, the UNODC/UNCTAD framework suggests that financial flows associated with tax avoidance should also be considered illicit where they cross borders. The report also notes that, while tax avoidance generally involves tax planning undertaken within the letter of the law, there is often substantial legal ambiguity over when aggressive tax planning becomes evasion. The line between evasion and avoidance can also be difficult to draw for statistical purposes where the legal environment around tax planning, particularly for MNEs, is changing rapidly. In such a context, the European Commission (2017[5]) suggests that the range of tax avoidance thus should be considered as a continuum of activities with fluid boundaries between legal tax planning and illegal tax evasion as the extremes.

The debate over whether tax avoidance should be included in the definition of IFFs remains highly contested. Fundamentally, suggesting that legal activities can be included in a definition of illicit activity introduces room for complexity, subjectivity and error into the IFF area which is not helpful for policy analysis or measurement. In the context of the SDG indicator and the underlying framework, tax avoidance, though generally considered legal, has been included as an IFF by UNODC/UNCTAD. However, strictly categorising tax avoidance or base erosion and profit shifting (BEPS) as IFFs may result in suggesting that legitimate economic activities associated with MNE investments are in fact illicit. This could include, for instance, MNEs funding investments in developing countries through debt financing, which would fall within the terms of current law. Such categorisation has the potential to conflate quite different policy challenges, which is unlikely to assist policy makers in properly diagnosing the problem and developing the appropriate policy response. It could also have the effect of diverting policy attention from other previously mentioned IFF categories, such as corruption, flows related to smuggling, trafficking, terrorist financing, exchange control contravention, and tax evasion. None of this is to understate the egregious nature of, or the extent to which tax avoidance is a problem, but it is a recognition of the difficulties that arise when tax avoidance is incorporated into the definition of IFFs. Automatically subsuming tax avoidance into IFFs may also lead to distorted IFF estimates as will be discussed further below. This is particularly the case when MNE activities have been the result of tax base choices made by countries. While the line between legal and illegal in the area of tax avoidance can often be contested by taxpayers and tax authorities, the line between licit and illicit forms of tax avoidance seems impossible to draw and is potentially highly subjective. This renders the challenge of accurately measuring IFFs even more difficult. For these reasons, this study excludes tax avoidance from its definition of IFFs.

Why are IFFs so harmful?

IFFs cause fiscal and economic damage to countries in a variety of ways. For developing countries in particular, tax- and customs-related IFFs often represent substantial amounts of lost or forgone tax revenue that could have otherwise been spent on reducing inequality and fighting poverty or fostering the structural transformation of their economies amid global challenges such as climate change. IFFs may also drain foreign exchange reserves, undercut legitimate trade and jeopardise the business environment. IFFs also undermine the investment base of a country. When capital leaves countries it undercuts their ability to finance development goals and invest in their economies. This may result in reduced scope and quality of public services, reduced public transfers or job creation, and ultimately, reduced confidence in public institutions.

Apart from the financial aspect, IFFs also undermine the trust of citizens. By evading taxes and channelling financial flows illicitly across borders, IFFs may undermine tax morale which may result in further erosion of the tax base, resulting in lower domestic tax compliance along with reduced cross-border tax compliance. IFFs often allow the proceeds of corruption and crime to flow overseas making it more challenging for authorities to tackle crime and reduce corruption. Assessing IFFs and successfully combatting financial leakages thus can not only improve domestic resource mobilisation but also support a government's social contract with its citizens and help achieve a more favourable business climate for private sector investment.

Existing IFF estimates and measurement challenges

Despite definitional challenges, because IFFs pose such significant risks to countries, there have been several attempts to estimate illicit flows on an international scale. The estimates are as heterogeneous as the methodologies applied and the underlying activities assumed to result in IFF-generating proceeds. For instance, in their most recent study based on trade data, GFI (2021[6]) estimate that total illicit flows from developing countries reached USD 1.6 trillion in 2018. While developing Asia accounted for around USD 390 billion or 25% of all flows, the African continent lost around USD 84 billion, accounting for 5% of global IFFs. For 2000 to 2008, AU/ECA (2015[7]) estimate cumulative IFFs from Africa due to trade mispricing of USD 162 billion, exhibiting an increasing trend over time. Other global estimates on criminal proceeds involving money laundering in 2009 amount to USD 2.1 trillion, an equivalent of about 3.5% of global GDP (UNODC, 2011[8]).

Other recent studies focus more on the global scale of individual tax evasion and offshore wealth. O'Reilly et al. (2019[9]) conduct an analysis into tax evasion and global offshore wealth in international financial centres (IFCs). They find that, based on bank account data from the BIS, global offshore wealth peaked at USD 2.5 trillion in 2008 and fell by around 42% to around USD 1.4 trillion until 2019. This drop in offshore deposits has largely been associated with the global expansion of tax transparency. Another study by Alstadsaeter et al. (2018[10]) reports that the stock of hidden offshore wealth has remained equal to about 10% of world GDP between 2001 and 2007. This order of magnitude corresponds to non-compliant foreign wealth of about USD 5.6 trillion in 2007.

Results for individual countries such as South Africa have very often been derived from the global or regional estimates. For instance, GFI (2021[6]) estimate average illicit outflows of around USD 20 billion for South Africa every year during 2009 - 2018. AU/ECA (2015[7]) suggests that South Africa's annual IFFs are around USD 14 billion, measured in terms of GDP and relative to financial market size. According to Signé et al. (2020[11]), the country emitted a total of USD 441.5 billion during the period from 1980 to 2018. This would result in average annual outflows of about USD 12 billion. Related to individual tax evasion, Alstadsaeter et al. (2018[10]) estimate South African total individual wealth in offshore destinations to amount to about USD 43.5 billion – an equivalent of 11.8% of South Africa's GDP in 2007.

However, the lack of a commonly agreed definition, inherent measurement challenges and the reliance on aggregated data render most IFF estimates imprecise and result in relatively high numbers. Moreover, studies following different approaches may estimate IFFs in ways that may or may not overlap. For example, studies based on trade-mispricing may also measure some IFFs associated with money laundering or tax evasion. Being aware of these challenges is therefore vital when trying to estimate and to interpret any results on IFFs.

Approaches to measuring IFFs

Measurement challenges in relation to IFFs arise in particular through their hidden nature. Due to being inherently secret, most conventional strategies to quantify IFFs by using existing data as, for instance, through surveys of households, businesses or financial institutions are unlikely to reveal IFFs. While some IFFs are remitted illicitly through the financial system, other IFFs (e.g. cross-border smuggling of cash) are not and need to be considered separately. Associating payments that are not illegal in their method of transfer with either domestic crime or corruption is challenging, as is associating payments that may have been earned and transferred legally with illicit use. As a result, IFF estimates often rely on proxies for illicit activity to estimate the size of IFFs. These approaches seldom allow for disaggregation of different kinds of IFFs into any of the subcategories in any of the frameworks discussed above.

The most commonly-cited measures of IFFs are generated using top-down estimation methods. This involves measuring IFFs using errors and asymmetries in aggregated macroeconomic data derived from global trade statistics, portfolio investment statistics or statistics on foreign direct investment. By exploiting mismatches in bilateral data series, however, these approaches often conflate statistical measurement problems with IFFs, potentially resulting in inflated numbers. For example, a common approach to measuring IFFs from trade mis-invoicing is to compare import data as recorded by Country A from Country B with export data as recorded by Country B to Country A. Where differences between these data exist, it is these asymmetries that are assumed to derive largely from IFFs. However, such discrepancies can also result from differences in the timing of imports and exports in statistics, differences in the categorisation of imports and exports by different countries, and simple measurement error (Collin, 2020[12]).

Some researchers have suggested that estimates based on mirror trade statistics may be unreliable due to these issues. In general, these challenges hail from the availability of suitable data, the overly general or mixed methods that are applied, the arbitrary and/or simplifying nature of the assumptions, the aggregation of categories, and a lack of the country-specific context when analysing and measuring IFFs (Nitsch, 2016[13]). Moreover, IFFs for individual countries are often simply derived from the global aggregate by accounting for a country's share in global trade or the regional economy as shown above.

In contrast, bottom-up methods to estimate IFFs rely on more granular micro-data, for instance from tax audits or individual tax returns. These methods try to identify the different individual IFF components and produce estimates for each, which may then be aggregated horizontally or from a lower to a higher level to obtain a national estimate. While they also differ in their degree of sophistication, the resulting accuracy of any estimate may be considered higher compared to the top-down estimation due to the reliance on microdata and activities that are directly related to the generation of IFFs.[2]

The second major challenge in measuring IFFs emerges from a lack of capacity or weak institutions to identify them in the first place. Developing countries, which very often face very significant IFF challenges, may lack reporting mechanisms or enforcement capacities to successfully detect and combat illicit outflows. For instance, the increasing reliance on tax data for the analysis of compliance demands data and analysis approaches that may strain the capacity of developing country tax administrations (Kennedy, 2019[14]). Developing countries have also been slower to benefit from progress in tax transparency, particularly due to resource constraints. This is particularly the case with respect to the CRS for AEOI, where many developing countries have not been able to put in place the required institutional processes to qualify to receive information. Out of the group of 108 jurisdictions that have committed to implement the standard by 2021, 32 are developing countries and 22 of them have started to reciprocally exchange to date (OECD, 2021[15]).

IFFs thus need to be analysed and measured in a country-specific context. They need to be considered in light of an economy's economic structure as well as its institutional environment and capacities. Differences therein not only determine IFF categories relevant in the specific context and their respective size but also the capacity of national authorities to effectively assess and combat any illicit outflows. Moreover, a country-specific perspective allows for a more tailored approach to estimating IFFs, likely using the kind of data best-suited to exploring a relevant IFF-generating activity. For these reasons while the estimates derived in Chapter 6 are estimates of all IFFs, much of the policy discussion in the present study concentrates on individual tax-related illicit flows as one major subcomponent of South Africa's IFF landscape.

Risks and sources of IFFs in South Africa

IFF risks in South Africa largely stem from its economic structure and geographic position. According to the recently concluded evaluation by FATF as well as consultations with national authorities, IFFs in South Africa are still considered a major threat to tax revenues and the overall economy – despite significant efforts undertaken and progress achieved.[3] IFFs can generally be divided into two large categories, namely flows pertaining to individuals and flows more closely related to corporates. While individual IFFs, for instance, consist to a large extent of direct transfers of funds, for example as the proceeds from illegal activities or funds wired offshore for the purpose of tax evasion, corporate IFFs are largely related to illegal trade activities. Inter-relationships and mutually reinforcing effects between the different categories exist and make them even harder to detect, demanding a more systemic view from authorities to combat IFFs successfully.

Tax offences with regard to income taxes have been characterised as being one of the most predominant forms of tax evasion (FATF, 2021[16]). Against this background, this report assesses one of the main elements of South Africa's IFF environment. The main domestic proceeds-generating crimes in South Africa have been identified as tax crimes, corruption and bribery, fraud, those linked to credit card abuse, and environmental and resource type crimes. Tax crimes encompass evasion of a broad range of taxes and fees, including corporate and personal income and customs and excise taxes as well as tax fraud (e.g. VAT fraud). Fraud includes Ponzi schemes, other investment, cyber-fraud, and digital banking frauds as well as those involving virtual assets. Criminal proceeds from these activities, income disguised as donations or gifts, or legal income earned are often illicitly channelled outside the country and into IFCs thereby contravening exchange control regulations. Given the criminality associated with the manner in which they are generated, such activities are unlikely to be tax compliant. They may also involve foreign investment allowances, crypto assets, financial emigration or funds that are transferred through Common Monetary Area (CMA) countries.

South Africa's geographic position as a key financial hub in the Southern African region and a relatively developed economy when compared to its neighbours potentially exposes it to the threat of foreign proceeds of crime, resulting in illicit in- and outflows. While funds can be laundered in or through South Africa from the region due to its relatively large financial sector, the country has also been described as a potential market and a transit point for trafficking in illicit goods, such as illicit drugs, or people smuggling. Corporate IFFs on the other hand are mostly related to trade mis-invoicing, commodities smuggling, transfer mispricing or advance payments (FATF, 2021[16]).[4]

> **Box 3.1. The challenge of tax avoidance in South Africa**
>
> Tax avoidance and activities related to base erosion and profit shifting (BEPS) by multinational enterprises (MNEs) are generally considered legal activities and should therefore not be included in the definition of IFFs. In spite of not being considered illicit in an IFF sense, BEPS activity is detrimental to a country's revenue collection capacity by diminishing its tax base. Activities considered as tax avoidance and BEPS were the focus of the OECD's *Action Plan on Base Erosion and Profit Shifting*, and the resulting OECD/G20 BEPS Project. The BEPS Project considered a range of tax avoidance behaviours, which included, for instance, the use of excessive interest payments, the strategic location of intangible assets and debt, the abuse of tax treaties and the manipulation of transfer pricing arrangements (OECD, 2013[17]).
>
> Developing countries in particular have been shown to be significantly exposed to tax avoidance. Research by Johannesen et al. (2020[18]), for instance, finds that the sensitivity of reported profits to profit-shifting incentives is negatively related to the level of economic and institutional development. The lack of fiscal capacity and the need for its improvement in many developing countries corroborate this view.
>
> South Africa is no exception in this regard. Tax avoidance activities have often been described as a major challenge and the estimated tax loss arising from it, in terms of revenues forgone, is substantial. For instance, one study showed that South African firms owned by a parent in an international financial centre (IFC) avoid taxation on as much as 80% of their true income (Wier and Reynolds, 2018[19]). However, not all tax-avoiding firms contribute equally to this aggregate tax loss. Most firms do not engage in tax avoidance, while the largest foreign-owned firms are found to contribute more strongly to overall estimated tax losses through tax avoidance strategies. Another study by Wier (2020[20]) estimates the tax loss related to imported goods alone at 0.5% of total corporate tax payments.
>
> The OECD has been at the forefront in the fight against tax avoidance. Important progress has been made in this policy area by the Inclusive Framework on BEPS, which brings together over 140 jurisdictions – the majority of them developing countries – on an equal footing to tackle tax avoidance. The BEPS package, released in October 2015 by OECD and G20 countries, delivers solutions for Governments to close the gaps in existing international rules that allow corporate profits to be artificially shifted to low or no tax jurisdictions where companies have little or no economic activity. The development of a multilateral instrument (MLI), an agreement to facilitate the implementation of the treaty-based BEPS measures, was concluded in 2016. As of February 2022, 99 countries of which 13 are African states, had signed the MLI.
>
> South Africa is an active member of the Inclusive Framework on BEPS (Inclusive Framework) and has also signed but not yet ratified the MLI. In line with MLI requirements, authorities spontaneously exchange information on rulings in relation to BEPS. Progress has also been made by the Inclusive Framework in improving the availability of data to support the measurement of tax avoidance by MNE groups, including through a regular public release of anonymised and aggregated country-by-country report statistics. South Africa has the legal framework for country-by-country reporting in place and exchanges actively. South Africa is also a member of the Steering Group of the Inclusive Framework, which has been examining income tax challenges associated with the digitalisation of the global economy, which delivered a landmark international tax agreement in October 2022.

South Africa's multilateral action against tax-related IFFs

Since the global financial crisis, the South African authorities have joined a number of multilateral tax transparency initiatives. While these initiatives have been part of the global effort to enhance tax compliance with respect to foreign source income, most of them have also been undertaken with the goal of mobilising government revenues. Most initiatives are thus related to countering tax-related IFFs such as tax evasion on a multilateral basis by facilitating the exchange of information (EOI) for tax purposes.

South Africa has been at the forefront on the African continent to join the global fight against tax-related IFFs. In 2009, the country became an early member of the Global Forum on Transparency and Exchange of Information for Tax Matters (the Global Forum). Signing the Convention on Mutual Administrative Assistance in Tax Matters (MAAC) in November 2011 expanded South African's information exchange network substantially. Established in 1988 and amended by Protocol in 2010 to allow for broader country participation, the MAAC not only provides for bilateral and multilateral EOI (including spontaneous exchange, EOIR, and AEOI[5]), it also includes assistance in recovery, the service of documents and can facilitate joint audits among its signatories. Moreover, the MAAC is not only a valuable tool for fighting tax evasion; it also has the potential to support other law enforcement purposes such as fighting corruption and money laundering (OECD/Council of Europe, 2011[21]). Over 140 jurisdictions have already joined the convention, broadening South Africa's network of exchange of information partners. Following the entry into force of the MAAC in early March 2014, South Africa also publicly committed to the early adoption of AEOI under the Common Reporting Standard (CRS) in May 2014. Joined by 44 other jurisdictions, the country announced the activation of automatic information exchange by 2017 with the first batch of taxpayer information having been exchanged in January the same year. As at March 2022, South Africa has 105 activated CRS agreements for partner jurisdictions to send CRS information.

Apart from global initiatives, increasing mutual assistance in tax matters in a developing country and regional context has become an important element in fighting tax evasion. Even prior to the introduction of the MAAC, the African Tax Administration Forum (ATAF) developed an EOI agreement open to signature by its members in 2012. The Agreement on Mutual Assistance in Tax Matters (AMATM) was set up to mutually provide ATAF member countries with tax information on a spontaneous or automatic basis or upon request.[6] Although twelve African countries have already signed the AMATM (Botswana, Eswatini, Gambia, Ghana, Lesotho, Liberia, Malawi, Mozambique, Nigeria, South Africa, Uganda and Zambia), and it has entered into force following ratification by four countries as required by the Agreement, only seven countries have so far ratified the AMATM (Gambia, Lesotho, Liberia, Mozambique, Nigeria, South Africa and Uganda). Moreover, on 17 August 2013, South Africa also signed a similar agreement between member countries of the Southern African Development Community (SADC), the Southern African Development Community's Agreement on Assistance in Tax Matters (SADCA). This agreement is not in force yet (AU/ATAF/OECD, 2021[22]).

South Africa has also been a founding member of the Africa Initiative, a programme created by the Global Forum to enhance EOI capacities among African countries. The Africa Initiative was launched in 2015 as a partnership between the Global Forum, its African members and a number of regional and international organisations and development partners: African Tax Administration Forum, Cercle de Réflexion et d'Échange des Dirigeants des Administrations Fiscales, World Bank Group, France (Ministry of Europe and Foreign Affairs) and the United Kingdom (Foreign, Commonwealth & Development Office). Since then, additional partners (African Development Bank, African Union Commission, European Union, Norway, Switzerland and the West African Tax Administration Forum) joined the initiative. The Africa Initiative is open to all African countries and currently has 33 African member jurisdictions. The Africa Initiative's work fits into broader agendas, as tax transparency is an opportunity to stem illicit financial flows and increase domestic resource mobilisation, which are central to the African Union Agenda 2063 and the Sustainable Development Goals (AU/ATAF/OECD, 2021[22]). Since 2021, South Africa has been the Vice-Chair of the Initiative.

The Africa Initiative has resulted in significant engagement at the ministerial level to ensure political buy-in and sustained momentum in the area of tax transparency. Initially set up for a period of three years (2015-2017), the Initiative was renewed for a second phase (2018-2020) in 2017 and for a third phase (2021-2023) in 2020. During the plenary a call for action was made through a landmark document, the "Yaoundé Declaration" which urges the African Union to begin a high-level discussion on tax cooperation and illicit financial flows and their link to domestic resource mobilisation. Supported by the OECD and the governments of France and the United Kingdom since its inception, this call for action to increase tax compliance, fight IFFs and foster domestic resource mobilisation has been signed by 33 signatories, including the African Union Commission. South Africa signed the declaration in September 2018 (OECD, 2021[23]).

Figure 3.2. Landmarks of tax transparency in South Africa over time

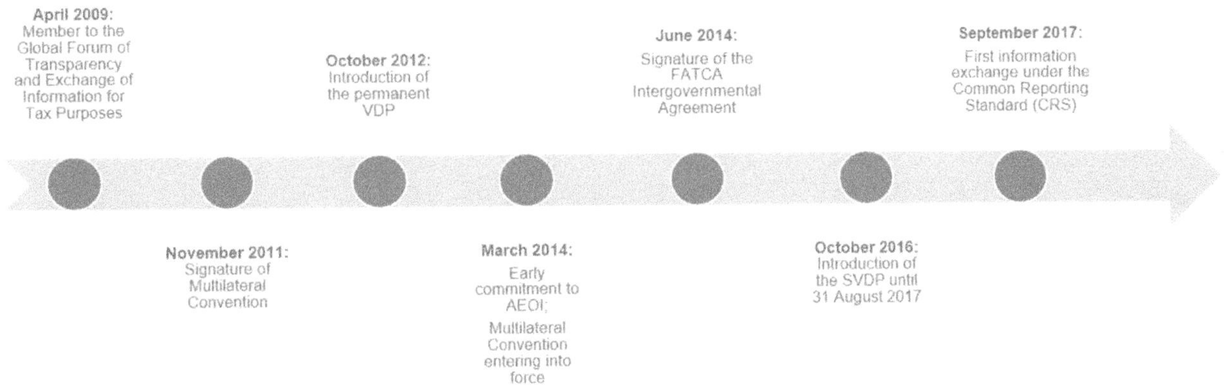

- April 2009: Member to the Global Forum of Transparency and Exchange of Information for Tax Purposes
- November 2011: Signature of Multilateral Convention
- October 2012: Introduction of the permanent VDP
- March 2014: Early commitment to AEOI; Multilateral Convention entering into force
- June 2014: Signature of the FATCA Intergovernmental Agreement
- October 2016: Introduction of the SVDP until 31 August 2017
- September 2017: First information exchange under the Common Reporting Standard (CRS)

Source: OECD Secretariat

Exchange of information (EOI)

The active exchange of information (EOI) between tax authorities can be considered the most effective way to enquire about offshore wealth and thus address tax evasion. The success of international tax co-operation, however, relies on the effective implementation of international standards. Successful implementation of EOI standards requires governments to ensure the availability of legal ownership information, beneficial ownership, accounting and banking information, the access to that information and its effective exchange with foreign partners, based on international agreements in force. The use of available exchange agreements in turn provides the government with a more comprehensive picture of its taxpayers' international financial affairs, their degree of compliance with domestic tax law and supports the fight against tax-related IFFs.

Adherents to the two internationally agreed standards on the exchange of information on request (EOIR) and of individual financial account information automatically (AEOI), are regularly monitored by the Global Forum to ensure effective implementation. As an early adherent to both standards, the country's institutional setting for EOI has been reviewed several times in the past. South Africa has implemented the necessary institutional requirements for successful implementation and operation of EOI (AU/ATAF/OECD, 2021[22]). The country's tax administration has an EOI strategy implemented. The EOI infrastructure in the form of a Competent Authority delegation, a dedicated EOI unit and staff as well as documentation procedures with database tracking tools have been in place. Moreover, revenue gains through EOI are monitored and additional taxes collected show that EOI has had a positive impact on revenue mobilisation in South Africa.

EOIR

Relative to most other African countries, South Africa's EOI network is wide with the possibility of exchanging information with more than 150 jurisdictions (OECD, 2021[24]). Over time, the country has entered into a large number of bilateral agreements, including through regional initiatives in Africa. Of the currently more than 100 bilateral agreements, the earliest entered into force in 1956 with Zambia (Figure 3.3). Since the mid-1990s the number of overall EOIR agreements has increased strongly, experiencing another surge after the global financial crisis due to the MAAC. The network of EOIR agreements with IFCs expanded later and has only recently experienced a substantial rise in bilateral relationships.

Figure 3.3. The expansion of South Africa's EOIR network over time, 1956 – 2019

Aggregated number of EOIR relationships of South Africa with all jurisdictions and IFCs only in force

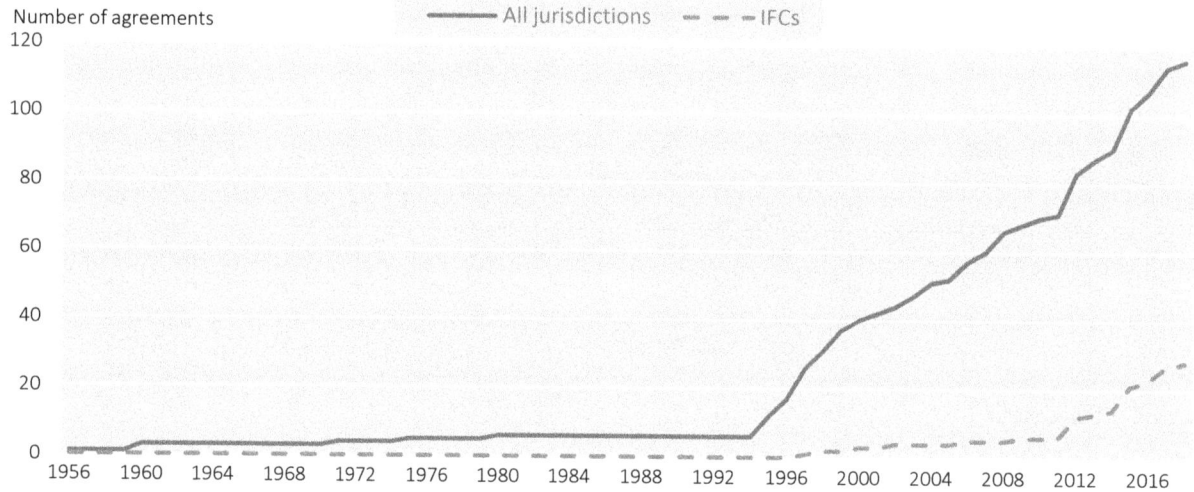

Source: Calculations based on OECD (2021[24]).

StatLink https://stat.link/7pak9t

South Africa has been reviewed on its implementation of the EOIR standard twice by the Global Forum, in 2012 and 2021. In 2012, South Africa was found compliant overall with regard to the 2010 Terms of Reference for both the legal implementation of the EOIR standard as well as its operation in practice (OECD, 2012[25]). Two recommendations were issued with regards to further developing its EOIR network and to better monitoring the availability of identity information related to partnerships. Since then, South Africa has implemented the first recommendation and now has a broad EOIR network, especially with the entry into force of the MAAC in 2014. Despite its sizeable network, however, requests through bilateral agreements have only been submitted sporadically to other jurisdictions.

In 2021, the new EOIR review has stressed the need for continued progress to ensure availability of beneficial ownership information as described in the second round of EOIR reviews. Due to a strengthening of the standard in 2016, the second review concludes that overall South Africa has a legal and regulatory framework "in place but needs improvement" regarding the availability of ownership, accounting and banking information as well as the quality and completeness of outgoing EOI requests (OECD, 2021[24]). In particular, improvements have been recommended with regards to the availability of regularly updated beneficial ownership information on all bank accounts and all relevant entities and arrangements. It also recommends South Africa to ensure that accounting information is available for a period of five years for all relevant companies, including those that redomicile out of the country.[7]

AEOI under the CRS

Following South Africa's public commitment to an early adoption of AEOI in 2014, exchanges have been taking place on an annual basis since 2017. Through the wide-spread adoption of the MAC, the global network of AEOI relationships has significantly increased within a relatively short period of time. South Africa signed the MAAC in 2014 and activated the associated CRS Multilateral Competent Authority Agreement (MCAA) in time for the first exchanges in 2017. To allow domestic financial institutions to collect and report the information to be exchanged, South Africa also amended the Tax Administration Act of 2011 and introduced CRS regulations (OECD, 2020[26]). As a result, South Africa currently has automatic information exchanges activated with 105 jurisdictions, 15 among them are in Africa, and more jurisdictions are expected to join the global network in the near future.

South Africa's legal framework for AEOI implementation was recently assessed during the AEOI peer review in November 2021 (OECD, 2021[27]). The quality of its confidentiality and data safeguards framework to ensure confidential exchange of data without the direct or indirect revelation of any taxpayer information under the CRS was assessed as fully compliant. The country's legal framework implementing the AEOI Standard was found to be in place and fully consistent with the requirements of the AEOI Terms of Reference. This includes South Africa's domestic legislative framework requiring Reporting Financial Institutions to conduct the due diligence and reporting procedures (core requirement 1) and its international legal framework to exchange the information with all of South Africa's Interested Appropriate Partners (core requirement 2). The Global Forum is currently reviewing South Africa's effectiveness in relation to AEOI in practice together with other jurisdictions with results due to be published by the end of 2022. Capacity development is progressing with 48 South African tax officials having participated in Global Forum training on EOI in 2020 (AU/ATAF/OECD, 2021[22]).

Domestic tax transparency initiatives in South Africa

During the last decade, voluntary disclosure programmes (VDPs) have become an internationally accepted practice to broaden the tax base and collect additional tax revenues across the world. Since 2009, over 90 VDPs have been implemented in more than 25 countries (O'Reilly, Parra Ramirez and Stemmer, 2019[9]). The programmes often differ significantly in terms of length and legal consequences of application. Moreover, the domestic implementation of voluntary disclosure has in the past often coincided with the signature of bilateral EOIR treaties or the commencement of AEOI.[8] As a result, many VDPs have encouraged taxpayers to declare non-compliant offshore deposits or repatriate hidden assets. Others have primarily targeted non-compliance with regards to other tax laws. South Africa has followed this path as well and introduced a total of 3 different VDPs since 2010. Depending on their targeted taxpayers and tax offences, the programmes have either been administered by SARS alone for tax defaults or in collaboration with SARB when dealing with contraventions of exchange control regulation due to undeclared offshore assets or foreign capital income.[9]

VDP

South Africa's first VDP was introduced on 27 October 2010 and lasted until 31 October 2011. The programme had a tax component, administered by SARS, and an exchange control component, administered by SARB's financial surveillance department. Taxpayers could thus either regulate their tax affairs, declare exchange control contraventions, or both by applying simultaneously to all programme components. Any tax default or exchange control contravention had to have occurred before the current tax year. While the main prerequisite for successful applications for tax defaults was that the information was not previously disclosed to SARS, SARB required detailed information of foreign assets and structures, their market value and whereabouts.[10] Successful applicants to SARS benefited from interest, penalty and additional tax relief; SARB did not impose administrative penalties. Criminal investigations were not initiated after full tax payment or full disclosure of contraventions.

One year later, SARS introduced a permanent VDP administered under the Tax Administration Act 28 of 2011 with effect from 1 October 2012. The general purpose of the programme is to enhance voluntary compliance in the interest of good management of the tax system and the best use of SARS resources (Republic of South Africa, 2012[28]). The VDP aims to encourage taxpayers to come forward on a voluntary basis to regularise their tax affairs and avoid the imposition of understatement penalties or other administrative fines. Penalties for late submission of returns are charged. Criminal prosecution will also not be initiated. The VDP is applicable to all taxes administered by SARS except for Customs and Excise. Both individuals and companies may apply to the programme provided they fulfil certain qualifying conditions.

As with the previous VDP, voluntary disclosure is required for a successful application. In the case of outstanding tax returns of which SARS has already been aware or where an investigation was already underway at the date of application, an application would be rendered void. Additional conditions include that the application must be formally completed and the application cannot result in a refund to the taxpayer. Upon approval of the application, an agreement is concluded between SARS and the applicant that reflects the outcome of the application process. A successful VDP assessment gives effect to the VDP agreement, and typically includes the disclosed additional taxable income and, depending on the length of time since the default occurred, interest and late payment penalties. In addition, the VDP allows for prospective applicants to make an initial "no-name" disclosure in order to obtain a non-binding opinion from SARS as to whether the applicant would qualify for relief and the extent of any relief.

SVDP

Alongside the VPD, National Treasury proposed a Special Voluntary Disclosure Programme (SVDP) in October 2016. Taxpayers with undisclosed offshore assets and foreign income only had a limited window for submissions from 1 October 2016 to 31 August 2017 to declare their contravention of exchange control regulation and tax default and apply for relief. With AEOI commencing in September 2017, the SVDP was implemented as a last-minute opportunity for non-compliant taxpayers to disclose their assets while at the same time using the threat of global detection to encourage applications. Taxpayers who missed this deadline could still make use of the normal VDP process to disclose offshore income.

The programme was administered by SARS and SARB and relief was offered relative to their competencies. The undeclared income that originally gave rise to the foreign asset was to be exempt from income tax, donations tax and estate duty liabilities that had arisen in the past. Only 40% of the highest value of the aggregate of all assets situated outside South Africa between (or deemed to be between) 1 March 2010 and 28 February 2015 that were derived from undeclared income were be included in taxable income and subject to tax in South Africa in the 2015 tax period. Investment earnings and other taxable events prior to 1 March 2015 were exempt from tax. Interest on tax debts arising from the disclosure only commenced from the 2015 year of assessment. Moreover, SARB charged different levies in contravention of exchange control regulations. Depending on a repatriation of funds, a 5% levy on the value of non-declared assets was imposed if assets were repatriated, with a 10% levy applying in case of non-repatriation. Levies had to be paid from foreign sourced funds. A levy of 12% arose if the 10% could not be paid from foreign sourced funds. Compared to previous VDPs, similar provisions applied with regards to criminal prosecution and the imposition of fines or administrative penalties (SARS, 2016[29]).

High-net worth individuals unit

Apart from increasing overall taxpayer compliance, high-net worth individuals (HNWIs) have been identified by SARS as important contributors to the South African economy but also as a potential source for IFFs. Their relatively high wealth and complexity of tax affairs may provide opportunities for aggressive tax planning and cross-border tax evasion. For these reasons, SARS established a stand-alone unit to monitor HNWI's compliance in 2008/09. Over time, the number of very wealthy individuals in South Africa's society has increased, together with their reported income. For instance, based on SARS statistics, Hundenborn, Woolard and Jellema (2019[30]) report an increase from 482 individuals with taxable income of more than ZAR 10 million in 2011 to 1048 individuals in 2014. During the same period, the maximum declared taxable income rose from ZAR 110 million to over ZAR 150 million.

Given their importance and potential revenue contribution, SARS attempted to provide a differentiated approach (treatment strategy) to ensure voluntary compliance. Individuals were classified as a HNWI based on a formal definition setting out a qualifying criteria. Since then, SARS' monitoring of this income tax segment has changed over time and various organisational formats have been tested. In 2015/16, the HNWI Unit was entirely disbanded with very few audits taking place in that year and the following year (Zondo Commission, 2022[31]).

After the National Treasury's announcement in February 2021, the High Wealth Individual (HWI) Unit re-started its operations with the aim to improve compliance of wealthy individuals. The new HWI Unit will have a limited focus on individuals with assets worth at least ZAR 75 million. At present its tax base consists of 1408 individuals (AU/ATAF/OECD, 2021[22]). Subsequently the SARS Commissioner announced the establishment of the HWI Taxpayer Segment to improve compliance of the identified individuals through a one-stop, superior service. The focus of the restructured HWI segment is to increase voluntary compliance of HWI taxpayers by providing clarity and certainty and making it easier to comply with their obligations, while at the same time improving SARS' ability to detect and respond to risks posed by the taxpayer segment. Having been receiving AEOI data on foreign financial accounts since 2017, EOI is expected to play a key role in the detection of possible non-compliance in relation to cross-border transactions and assets held offshore.

References

Alstadsaeter, A., N. Johannesen and G. Zucman (2018), "Who owns the wealth in tax havens? Macro evidence and implications for global inequality", *Journal of Public Economics*, Vol. 162, pp. 89-100, https://doi.org/10.1016/j.jpubeco.2018.01.008. [10]

Andersson, J., F. Schroyen and G. Tosvik (2019), *The impact of international tax information exchange agreements on the use of tax amnesty: evidence from Norway*, https://papers.ssrn.com/sol3/Delivery.cfm/SSRN_ID3463645_code1391513.pdf?abstractid=3463645&mirid=1. [32]

AU/ATAF/OECD (2021), *Tax Transparency in Africa 2021 - Africa Initiative Progress Report*, OECD Publishing, https://www.oecd.org/tax/transparency/documents/Tax-Transparency-in-Africa-2021.pdf. [22]

AU/ECA (2015), *Track it! Stop it! Get it! Report of the High Level Panel of Illicit Financial Flows from Africa*, https://repository.uneca.org/bitstream/handle/10855/22695/b11524868.pdf?sequence=3&isAllowed=y. [7]

Baker, R. (2005), *Capitalism's Achilles Heel: Dirty Money and How to Renew the Free-Market System*, Wiley. [1]

Collin, M. (2020), "Illicit Financial Flows: Concepts, Measurement, and Evidence", *The World Bank Research Observer*, Vol. 35/1, pp. 44-86, https://doi.org/10.1093/wbro/lkz007. [12]

European Commission (2017), *Aggressive tax planning indicators – Final Report*, Publications Office of the European Union, https://doi.org/10.2778/847061. [5]

FATF (2021), *Anti-money laundering and counter-terrorist financing measures – South Africa, Fourth Round Mutual Evaluation Report*, FATF, http://www.fatf-gafi.org/publications/mutualevaluations/documents/mer-south-africa-2021.html. [16]

Global Financial Integrity (2021), *Trade-Related Illicit Financial Flows in 134 Developing Countries: 2009-2018*, https://secureservercdn.net/50.62.198.97/34n.8bd.myftpupload.com/wp-content/uploads/2021/12/IFFs-Report-2021.pdf?time=1643653304. [6]

Hundenborn, J., I. Woolard and J. Jellema (2019), "The effect of top incomes on inequality in South Africa", *International Tax and Public Finance*, Vol. 26, pp. 1018-1047, https://doi.org/10.1007/s10797-018-9529-9. [30]

Johannesen, N., T. Torslov and L. Wier (2020), "Are Less Developed Countries More Exposed to Multinational Tax Avoidance? Method and Evidence from Micro-Data", *The World Bank Economic Review*, Vol. 34/3, pp. 790-809, https://doi.org/10.1093/wber/lhz002. [18]

Kennedy, S. (2019), "The potential of tax microdata for tax policy", *OECD Taxation Working Papers*, No. 45, OECD Publishing, Paris, https://dx.doi.org/10.1787/d2283b8e-en. [14]

Nitsch, V. (2016), *Trillion dollar estimate: Illicit financial flows from*, http://nbn-resolving.de/urn:nbn:de:tuda-tuprints-54379. [13]

O'Reilly, P., K. Parra Ramirez and M. Stemmer (2019), "Exchange of information and bank deposits in international financial centres", *OECD Taxation Working Papers*, No. 46, OECD Publishing, Paris, https://dx.doi.org/10.1787/025bfebe-en. [9]

OECD (2021), *Global Forum on Transparency and Exchange of Information for Tax Purposes - Reinforcing Multilateral Co-operation in Tax Matters for a Fair and Inclusive Recovery (2021 Global Forum Annual Report)*, OECD Publishing, https://www.oecd.org/tax/transparency/documents/global-forum-annual-report-2021.pdf. [15]

OECD (2021), *Global Forum on Transparency and Exchange of Information for Tax Purposes: South Africa 2021 (Second Round, Phase 1): Peer Review Report on the Exchange of Information on Request*, Global Forum on Transparency and Exchange of Information for Tax Purposes, OECD Publishing, Paris, https://dx.doi.org/10.1787/fed716dd-en. [24]

OECD (2021), *Peer Review of the Automatic Exchange of Financial Account Information 2021*, OECD Publishing, Paris, https://dx.doi.org/10.1787/90bac5f5-en. [27]

OECD (2021), *The Yaoundé Declaration*, OECD Publishing, https://www.oecd.org/tax/transparency/what-we-do/technical-assistance/Yaounde-Declaration-with-Signatories.pdf. [23]

OECD (2020), *Peer Review of the Automatic Exchange of Financial Account Information 2020*, OECD Publishing, Paris, https://dx.doi.org/10.1787/175eeff4-en. [26]

OECD (2013), *Action Plan on Base Erosion and Profit Shifting*, OECD Publishing, Paris, https://dx.doi.org/10.1787/9789264202719-en. [17]

OECD (2012), *Global Forum on Transparency and Exchange of Information for Tax Purposes - Peer Reviews: South Africa*, OECD Publishing, Paris, https://dx.doi.org/10.1787/2219469x. [25]

OECD/Council of Europe (2011), *The Multilateral Convention on Mutual Administrative Assistance in Tax Matters: Amended by the 2010 Protocol*, OECD Publishing, Paris, https://dx.doi.org/10.1787/9789264115606-en. [21]

Republic of South Africa (2012), *Government Gazette, 4 July 2012*, https://www.gov.za/sites/default/files/gcis_document/201409/a282011.pdf. [28]

SARS (2016), *External Guide - Special Voluntary Disclosure Programme*, https://www.sars.gov.za/wp-content/uploads/Ops/Guides/GEN-VDP-02-G02-Special-Voluntary-Disclosure-Programme-External-Guide.pdf. [29]

Signé, L., M. Sow and P. Madden (2020), *Illicit financial flows in Africa: Drivers, destinations, and policy options*, https://www.brookings.edu/wp-content/uploads/2020/02/Illicit-financial-flows-in-Africa.pdf. [11]

UNECA (2013), *The State of Governance in Africa: The Dimension of Illicit Financial Flows as a Governance Challenge. Third ECA Meeting of the Committee on Governance and Popular Participation (CGPP)*, United Nations Publishing, https://repository.uneca.org/handle/10855/22142. [2]

UNODC (2011), *Estimating illicit financial flows resulting from drug trafficking and other transnational organized crimes*, https://www.unodc.org/documents/data-and-analysis/Studies/Illicit_financial_flows_2011_web.pdf. [8]

UNODC/UNCTAD (2020), *Conceptual Framework for the Statistical Measurement of Illicit Financial Flows*, https://www.unodc.org/documents/data-and-analysis/statistics/IFF/IFF_Conceptual_Framework_for_publication_15Oct.pdf. [4]

Wier, L. (2020), "Tax-motivated transfer mispricing in South Africa: Direct evidence using transaction data", *Journal of Public Economics*, Vol. 184, pp. 1-16, https://doi.org/10.1016/j.jpubeco.2020.104153. [20]

Wier, L. and H. Reynolds (2018), *Big and "unprofitable"*, https://www.wider.unu.edu/sites/default/files/Publications/Working-paper/PDF/wp2018-111.pdf. [19]

World Bank (2017), *Domestic Resource Mobilization and Illicit Financial Flows - Board Update*, https://documents1.worldbank.org/curated/en/877291492623853466/pdf/IFFs-DRM-Board-Note-Master-vFINAL-04102017.pdf. [3]

Zondo Commission (2022), *Judicial Commission of Inquiry into State Capture Report: Part 1 - Volume 1: South African Airways and its Associated Companies*, https://www.statecapture.org.za/site/files/announcements/638/Judicial_Commission_of_Inquiry_into_State_Capture_Report:_Part_1_Vol._1:_SAA_(18_MB).pdf. [31]

Notes

[1] This means a significant reduction of IFFs as stated in SDG target 16.4.

[2] Consult, for instance, Collin (2020[12]) for a more detailed view on IFF measurement challenges and Kennedy (2019[14]) on the importance of microdata.

[3] Comments by participants expressed during consultations on South Africa's IFF risks with National Treasury, SARS, the Financial Intelligence Unit, the Reserve Bank, as well as FATF and academics are gratefully acknowledged.

[4] Transfer mispricing has been analysed in detail from the South African perspective by Wier (2020[20]).

[5] This standard in AEOI requires the automatic exchange each year of information collected and reported by Financial Institutions on the financial accounts and assets they maintain for non-resident taxpayers.

[6] The text to the Agreement is available at: https://events.ataftax.org/includes/preview.php?file_id=46&language=en_US.

[7] As the COVID-19 pandemic prevented the holding of any onsite visits to South Africa, the 2021 review is limited to the adequacy of the legal and regulatory framework of South Africa to the standard of transparency and exchange of information on request. The review of the implementation of that framework in practice is scheduled to take place in 2022.

[8] Norway, for instance, implemented a VDP prior to tax exchange agreements with Luxembourg and Switzerland (Andersson, Schroyen and Tosvik, 2019[32]).

[9] Details of the impact of these programmes are discussed in Chapter 5.

[10] Information has been retrieved from: https://www.sars.gov.za/wp-content/uploads/Docs/MediaReleases/2010/SARS-MR-2010-053-Media-release-on-SARS-and-SARB-for-the-Voluntary-Disclosure-Programme-5-November-2010.pdf.

4 The tax system in South Africa

Key messages

- This chapter takes a closer look at South Africa's tax system and the development of its tax mix over time.
- South Africa's tax base is relatively broad compared to most middle-income countries but is narrow by comparison with OECD countries.
- South Africa's tax system tends to increasingly rely on direct taxes and in particular on income taxes.
- This reliance bears risks to the tax base and requires a well-functioning tax system that ensures compliance.

Introduction

This chapter provides an overview of the South African tax policy environment. It discusses the overall tax system, how it compares to similar jurisdictions, focusing in particular on developments in the tax mix and the country's strong reliance on direct taxes.[1]

An overview of the South African tax system

South Africa's tax base is relatively broad compared to most other middle-income countries, but is narrow by comparison to the OECD average. Its composition of tax revenues resembles, to a certain extent, that of OECD countries (Figure 4.1). The country derives about 60% of its total tax revenue from direct taxes. Roughly two-thirds of direct taxes (34% of total taxes) come from personal income taxes. In contrast, personal income taxes tend to comprise a lower share of overall tax revenue in other African economies, reflecting the sizeable informal sectors and low capacity in many of these countries. Taxes on goods and services account for a larger share in most countries than in South Africa. The variation in social security contributions (SSCs) reflects the diversity of social security systems and contribution rates as many countries use a variety of systems to fund social security benefits. For instance, SSCs in South Africa are comparatively small, with a 2% contribution rate levied on wages to finance the Unemployment Insurance Fund. Other benefits, such as social assistance programmes covering old age, sickness and maternity, are financed by general revenues.

Figure 4.1. The tax mix in South Africa compared to African and OECD countries in 2018

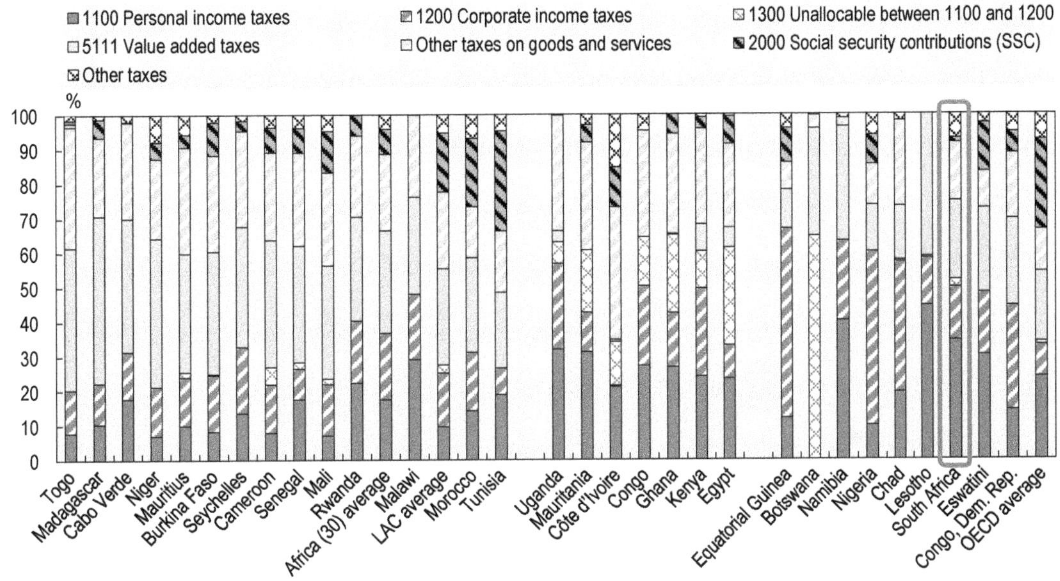

- 1100 Personal income taxes
- 1200 Corporate income taxes
- 1300 Unallocable between 1100 and 1200
- 5111 Value added taxes
- Other taxes on goods and services
- 2000 Social security contributions (SSC)
- Other taxes

Note: Figures include sub-national government tax revenues for Eswatini, Mauritania, Mauritius, Morocco, Nigeria (state revenues only) and South Africa for 2018. The Africa (30) average, the averages for LAC (25 Latin American and Caribbean countries) and the OECD (36 countries) are unweighted. The Africa (30) average should be interpreted with caution as data for social security contributions are not available or are partial in a few countries. See the country tables in Chapter 5 for further information. Botswana: The breakdown of revenue from income tax by personal income tax and corporate income tax is not available. OECD average: The data are for 2017 as data for 2018 are not available.
Source: OECD staff calculations based on data from (OECD/AUC/ATAF, 2020[1]), "Revenue Statistics in Africa: Comparative tables", OECD Tax Statistics (database), https://dx.doi.org/10.1787/be755711-en.

StatLink https://stat.link/g8psnx

Income taxes in South Africa

Since 2001, South African residents have been subject to income tax on their worldwide income and gains, and non-residents have been taxed on their South African sourced income and gains. The switch from a territorial to a residence-based tax system was aimed at broadening the country's tax base. The tax period for income tax (year of assessment), is generally 1 March to the end of February of the subsequent year. The South African tax system is based on individual tax filings. All formal employees must be registered by their employer for personal income tax, which is then deducted at source. An employer is obliged by law to issue tax certificates (IRP5) to all its employees to complete their income tax return after payroll reports have been submitted to SARS. The IRP5 certificate contains all the remuneration (including allowances and benefits) provided by an employer to the employee during a tax year. Moreover, a separate tax certificate (ITR12) exists for income and certain tax source other than a single employment income. This certificate is required for employment income from more than one source, investment income above exempt thresholds and foreign capital income or if additional deductions to taxable income are claimed.[2]

During the last decade, South Africa's share of direct taxes in overall tax receipts has increased. Amid a rising tax-to-GDP ratio during 2010 to 2018, the contributing share of income, profit and capital gains taxes increased by 1.7 percentage points. This increase exceeded developments for other tax types and also outpaced the respective growth of direct taxes in other African economies (Figure 4.2). The relative increase in tax-to-GDP ratios across the BRICS and the OECD was also lower. While South

Africa's growing tax revenues can generally be considered positive given its challenging fiscal situation, the increasing reliance on direct taxes as the dominant source of revenue highlights the importance of supporting income tax compliance.

Figure 4.2. Net changes in tax-to-GDP ratios for South Africa and selected countries, 2010 - 2019

Changes in main types of taxes are expressed in percentage point (p.p.) changes

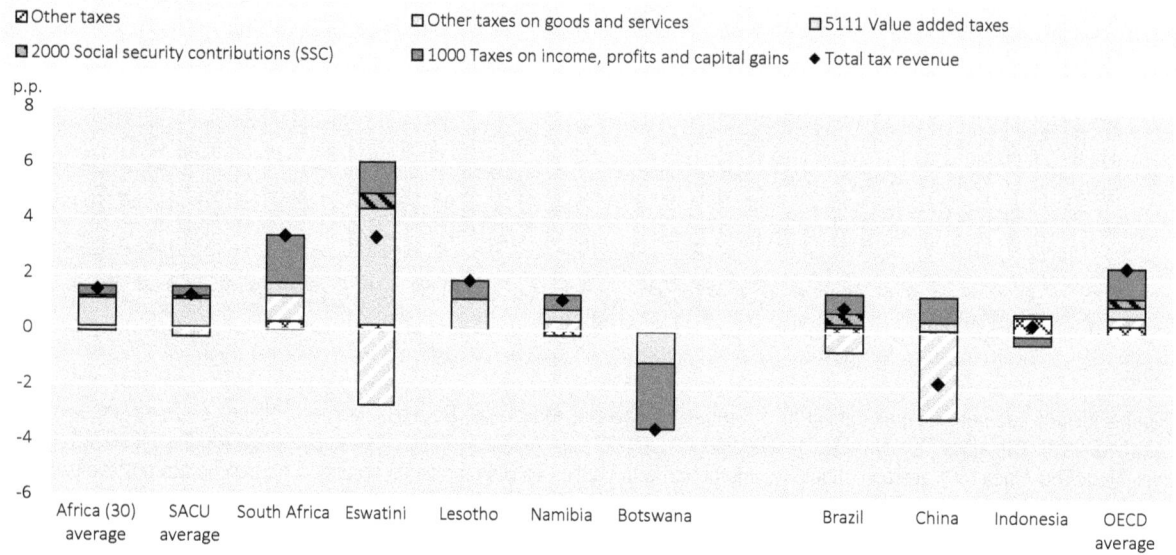

Note: Figures for African countries and the OECD average are based on 2018 data. Changes to the total tax revenue for China and Indonesia are shown exclusive of social security contributions.
Source: Calculations by OECD staff based on the OECD Revenue Statistics database.

StatLink https://stat.link/0sbyep

This trend is also reflected in South Africa's relatively high contribution of income tax to the overall tax share in total labour costs (Figure 4.3). At around 14.5%, income tax as a share of total labour costs in South Africa far exceeds that of its emerging market peers (OECD, 2021[2]). In Brazil, China, India and Indonesia, employees at the average wage pay no or little income tax and employer SSCs, which account for between 50% to 80% of the tax wedge.[3] While South Africa's income tax share in labour costs is also larger than the OECD average, the difference of 1.2% is relatively small. Employee and employer SSCs, however, account for significantly larger shares across OECD countries. Given South Africa's reliance on direct taxes, a well-functioning income tax system is therefore central to ensuring compliance and enabling reliable revenue collection.

Figure 4.3. Income tax plus employees' and employers' social security contributions, 2019

Expressed as % of labour costs

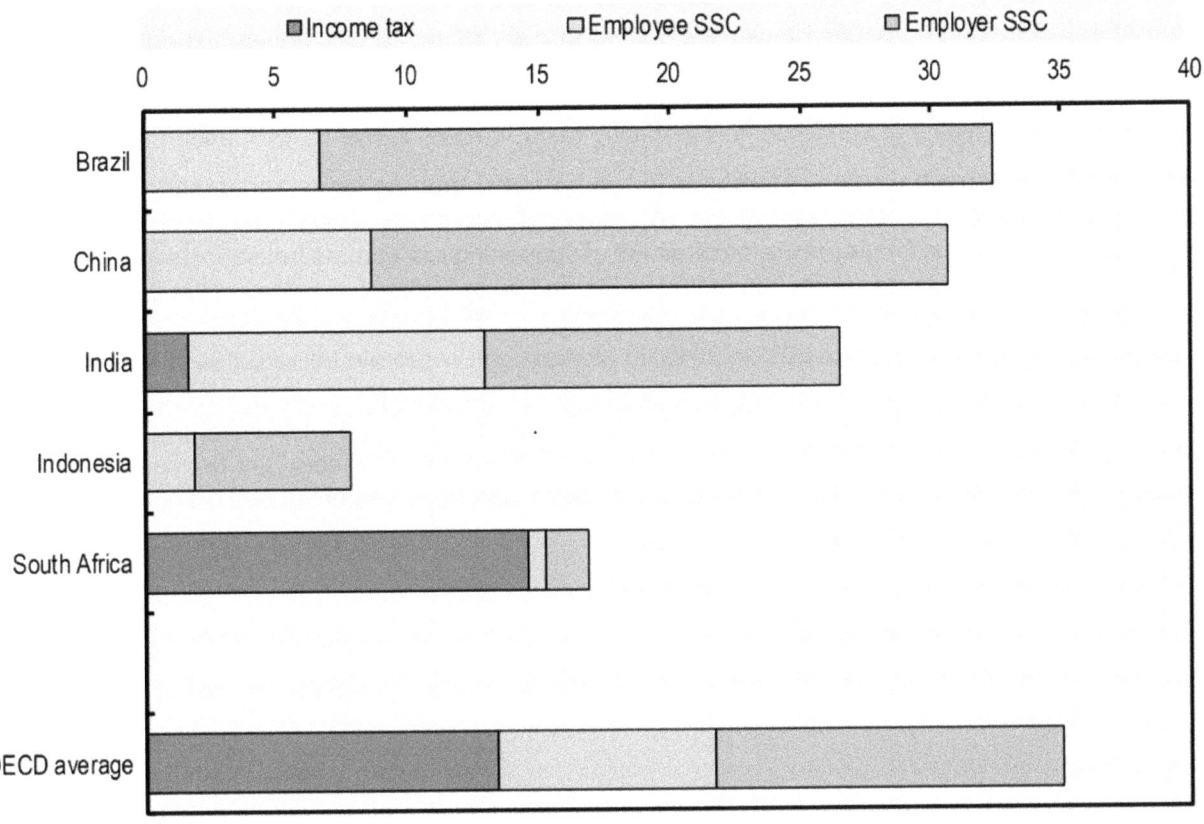

Note: Single individual without children at the income level of the average worker. The scenario for India includes SSCs only when payable. Payroll taxes are included where applicable.
Source: Adapted from "Taxing Wages in selected partner economies: Brazil, China, India, Indonesia and South Africa in 2019", https://www.oecd.org/tax/tax-policy/taxing-wages-in-selected-partner-economies.pdf.

Individuals are taxed at progressive rates. As of 1 March 2022, income tax rates range from 18% on taxable income up to ZAR 226 000 with a maximum marginal tax rate of 45% on taxable income above ZAR 1 731 600. Trusts are taxed at a flat rate of 45% except for special trusts, which have been created for the benefit of a person with special needs and are taxed at the 18% - 45% progressive rate. A tax-free allowance below which no tax return needs to be filed has increased over time and currently stands at ZAR 91 250. This income tax allowance increases for taxpayers above the age of 65. In an effort to promote saving, interest income from a domestic source is tax-exempt up to ZAR 23 800 for taxpayers younger than 65 and up to ZAR 34 500 for an age of 65 and older. Individuals in receipt of income other than remuneration in excess of prescribed thresholds, trusts, and companies pay tax under a presumptive tax system. Dividends earned by individuals from South African companies are generally exempt from the progressive income tax, but a 20% dividends tax is withheld at the company level. Individual income from foreign dividends through shareholding in foreign companies is taxable at a rate of 20% at the personal level (SARS, 2022[3]).

Companies, both resident and non-resident, are currently taxed at a standard corporate income tax rate of 28%. Companies are considered resident if they are incorporated or if they have their place of effective management in South Africa. Non-resident companies that do not have their place of effective management in South Africa are subject to source-based income tax. Resident small businesses and micro firms are taxed at lower and progressive rates. Small business corporations are taxed at progressive rates, which, from 1 April 2022, range from 0% on taxable income up to ZAR 91 250 with a maximum tax rate of 28% on taxable income above ZAR 550 000 (SARS, 2022[3]). Micro firms are taxed at progressive rates on taxable turnover. From 1 March 2022, the tax rate ranges from 0% on taxable turnover up to ZAR 335 000 with a maximum tax rate of 3% on taxable turnover above ZAR 750 000. A qualifying micro firm's turnover may not exceed ZAR 1 000 000, although discretion exists whereby SARS may permit a nominal and temporary excess. Tax is paid at the company level, and again at the shareholder level when profits are distributed, by means of the dividend withholding tax discussed above (SARS, 2022[3]).

Recent developments have seen increases in top personal income taxes and declines in corporate income taxes. During recent years, these top personal income tax (PIT) rates have been adjusted upwards several times to finance tax reforms aimed at supporting low-income households (OECD, 2020[4]). In 2017, the top PIT rate was raised from 41% to 45% and below-inflation adjustments in the brackets and allowances have been made for a number of years (Figure 4.4). In addition, the dividends tax, introduced in 2012 at 15%, was increased to 20% in 2017. In contrast, the corporate tax rate has followed the global decline in rates and has been cut several times over the last two decades. Having stood at 38.5% in 2001, the rate was reduced to 28% in 2013 after a number of decreases in the intervening period.[4] Instead of increasing the personal income tax further, the government seeks to broaden the tax base in the future through higher economic growth, increasing employment and better enforcement (National Treasury of South Africa, 2021[5]).

Figure 4.4. Tax trends in South Africa over time

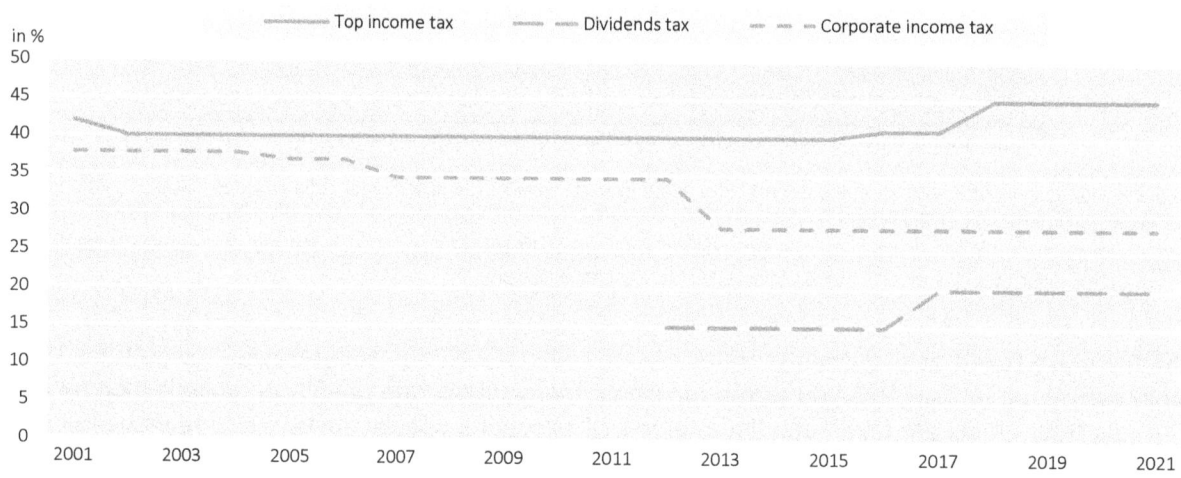

Note: Dividends tax was first introduced on 1 April 2012. Maximum effective tax rate to capital gains is 18%. 40% of net capital gains are taxed at the normal income tax rates.
Source: SARS and SARB, 2021.

StatLink https://stat.link/24u896

Due to South Africa's high inequality and the tax-free threshold, only about 40% of South Africa's working-age population (for adults of age 20 and above) are required to file income tax returns. These taxpayers tend to belong to the high-income segments of the income distribution. During the last decade, the number of officially registered taxpayers has grown annually by around 7.5% despite rising compulsory submission thresholds. Most taxpayers who are below the submission threshold are therefore not liable to file a tax return, but some may nonetheless do so to recover tax deducted (National Treasury/SARS, 2020[6]). Official estimates by SARS of expected returns submitted by registered taxpayers have, however, remained relatively stable over time (National Treasury/SARS, 2020[6]).

References

National Treasury of South Africa (2021), *Budget Review 2021*, http://www.treasury.gov.za/documents/National%20Budget/2021/review/FullBR.pdf. [5]

National Treasury/SARS (2020), *2020 Tax Statistics*, https://www.sars.gov.za/wp-content/uploads/Docs/TaxStats/2020/Tax-Statistics-2020.pdf. [6]

OECD (2021), *Taxing Wages in selected partner economies: Brazil, China, India, Indonesia and South Africa in 2019*, OECD Publishing, https://www.oecd.org/tax/tax-policy/taxing-wages-in-selected-partner-economies.pdf. [2]

OECD (2020), *Tax Policy Reforms 2020: OECD and Selected Partner Economies*, OECD Publishing, Paris, https://dx.doi.org/10.1787/7af51916-en. [4]

OECD (forthcoming), *OECD Economic Surveys: South Africa 2022*, OECD Publishing. [7]

OECD/AUC/ATAF (2020), *Revenue Statistics in Africa 2020*, OECD Publishing, https://doi.org/10.1787/14e1edb1-en-fr. [1]

SARS (2022), *Budget Tax Guide 2022*, https://www.sars.gov.za/wp-content/uploads/Docs/Budget/2022/Budget-Tax-Guide-2022.pdf. [3]

Notes

[1] South Africa's tax policies are discussed further in the forthcoming OECD Economic Surveys: South Africa 2022 (OECD, forthcoming[7]).

[2] These different forms of taxpayer filing will be discussed further in Chapter 5.

[3] The tax wedge is defined the difference between total labour compensation paid by the employer and the net take-home pay of employees, as a share of total labour compensation.

[4] The data are based on the combined corporate tax rate from the OECD Tax Database. For South Africa, these figures for the corporate tax rate include both South Africa's statutory corporate tax rate as well as the Secondary Tax on Companies which in South Africa was converted to a dividends tax in 2012.

5 Taxpayer responses to increasing tax transparency in South Africa

Key messages

- This chapter analyses taxpayer behaviour amid a variety of tax transparency initiatives implemented in South Africa.
- Tax evasion is shown to have a long history and has been concentrated among the very wealthy and top income earners.
- International financial centres (IFCs) have been the priority destinations for hiding non-compliant wealth abroad.
- Taxpayers have responded to multilateral tax transparency initiatives such as the implementation of the Common Reporting Standard (CRS).
- Strong increases in tax filings in relation to foreign capital income and previously undisclosed amounts of foreign capital income by new taxpayers are evidence of a strong CRS impact on tax revenues.
- The responsiveness by taxpayers to domestic transparency initiatives such as voluntary disclosure programmes has also been triggered by the implementation of the CRS.
- Improving the use of exchanged data, and the more effective use of bilateral information exchange treaties with IFCs should be key priorities.

Introduction

This chapter analyses tax evasion by assessing tax compliance amid a variety of tax transparency initiatives implemented in South Africa.[1] It first provides an overview of the literature regarding the characteristics of cross-border tax evasion and undeclared offshore wealth. This review presents useful evidence from various countries for the subsequent data analysis by assessing the effectiveness of domestic tax transparency initiatives and by examining income and wealth characteristics of participants in these initiatives. The subsequent section introduces the different data sources in more detail. After outlining the different approaches of the quantitative analysis, the chapter embarks on an assessment of taxpayer responsiveness to tax transparency initiatives – based on tax return filings over time and an individual in-depth evaluation of South Africa's VDP and SVDP programmes. A more detailed analysis of foreign financial account information exchanged under the CRS is provided in the next chapter.

How income distribution and foreign capital income matter for tax evasion and undeclared offshore wealth in South Africa

Cross-border tax evaders and holders of non-compliant offshore wealth tend to belong to the very top of the income and wealth distribution. Recent evidence across various countries shows that individual tax evasion increases with wealth and income levels. These stylised facts have largely been discovered through taxpayer responsiveness to VDPs. Colombian taxpayers, for instance, who have disclosed their hidden assets in the Colombian government's VDP belong to the very top of the country's wealth distribution. Moreover, the magnitude of disclosures appears to rise with the wealth level. While the top 0.5% confessed to hiding 28% of their wealth, the top 0.01% kept 37.5% of their net worth hidden abroad (Londoño-Vélez and Ávila-Mahecha, 2021[1]). In a similar vein, Alstadsaeter, Johannesen and Zucman (2019[2]) conduct an investigation into tax evasion for Scandinavian countries and find widespread evasion among those taxpayers with high wealth levels. In Norway and Sweden, the 0.01% richest households evade about 25% of their taxes owed. By assessing taxpayers' responsiveness to a tax amnesty programme from the Dutch authorities, Leenders et al. (2020[3]) report a similar concentration of tax evasion at the top.

While domestic compliance initiatives provide an improved sense of cross-border tax evasion by well-off taxpayers and encourage the disclosure of hidden assets, some evidence nonetheless suggests that the wealthiest evaders can be less affected. Leenders et al. (2020[3]) document a muted reaction to the Dutch amnesty programme by high-income evaders, which was in part ascribed to sophisticated evasion schemes and little incentives to come forward in terms of attenuated fines. The analysis on US taxpayers by Johannesen et al. (2020[4]) puts VDP participants predominantly in the top 10% of the income distribution, while noting that they very rarely belong to the highest income percentiles. By relying on new data from random audits in the United States, Guyton et al. (2021[5]) report that detected evasion declines sharply at the very top of the income distribution, with only a trivial amount of evasion detected in the top 0.1%. Moreover, they find that random audits capture tax evasion through offshore accounts and pass-through businesses only to a very limited extent. These two channels are both quantitatively important for the top 1%. These results are consistent with the observations by Harrington (2016[6]) who reports that non-compliant offshore accounts held by high-income taxpayers are often held in IFC jurisdictions. A mere reliance on VDPs thus appears to distort estimates of offshore assets, leaving tax evasion by the most well-off often considerably underestimated.

Assessing capital income derived from assets held abroad can also be considered a viable strategy for analysing taxpayer responses to tax enforcement initiatives. Existing studies have shown that taxes on capital income may present higher tax evasion risks relative to other forms of income (e.g. Londoño-Vélez and Ávila-Mahecha (2021[1]); Leenders et al. (2020[3])). In gauging the response of capital income reporting to enforcement initiatives, Johannesen et al. (2020[4]) assess reported foreign capital income in the form of interest, dividends and capital gains from offshore bank accounts of US citizens residing abroad. The largest share of these accounts are located in IFCs. As shown by Guyton et al. (2021[5]), under-reporting detected through random audits in the United States particularly applies to interest, dividends and capital gains.

Higher income taxpayers tend to earn more capital income from abroad. The share of capital income from domestic and foreign investments in taxable income tends to rise with a taxpayer's position in the overall income distribution. Financial capital income and business income, despite the limits of detection strategies, particularly gain importance as sources of income at the top (Guvenen, Kaplan and Song, 2014[7]; Guyton et al., 2021[5]). In South Africa, for instance, the capital share rises slowly from 15 to 20 percent between the 95th and 99th percentiles, before rapidly increasing to more than half of total income on average for the top percentile of the distribution (Bassier and Woolard, 2020[8]). Similar evidence has been found for the United Kingdom (Advani and Summers, 2020[9]). Recent evidence from Norway further shows that the dominant financial wealth components in the top percentiles are, among others, assets held abroad (Fagareng et al., 2020[10]). The concentration of foreign capital income at the top across countries thus suggests that an assessment of the size of tax evasion and the amount of non-compliant wealth held offshore is linked to an analysis of the relationship between income and wealth levels at the top and the contribution of foreign capital income to total taxable income.

Income and wealth is highly concentrated among the top percentiles in South Africa (Chatterjee, Czajka and Gethin, (2020[11]); Hundenborn, Woolard and Jellema, (2019[12])). Orthofer (2016[13]) reports a strong correlation between income and wealth in the highest income percentiles. There is also evidence of a widespread reliance on trusts and similar investment funds by the higher-income segment of the South African population as a means of investing in financial assets (Chatterjee, Czajka and Gethin, 2020[11]). For instance, more than half of total investment in bonds and stocks is held through trusts by the upper end of the wealth distribution.[2] These patterns suggest that most of the assets held abroad and foreign income derived from these assets belong to the very top of the income distribution in South Africa. Undeclared foreign capital income can be considered as a product of the accumulation of foreign wealth by individual financial outflows in the past. For this reason, the analysis below will largely focus on tax data of foreign capital income from interest, dividends and capital gains and focus on the top segments of the income distribution in assessing the impact of compliance initiatives.

Data

The analysis in this report relies on anonymised South African taxpayer data.[3] The data includes anonymised individual tax records comprising various sources of taxable income, tax returns on foreign investment income and detailed data from participants in the VDP and the SVDP, as well as data on information exchanged under the CRS.

Tax microdata has a couple of advantages compared to survey data in assessing tax compliance. Due to its administrative nature, this data usually covers the full tax-paying population. As it is not a sample, it identifies all individual taxpayers, which greatly increases the granularity of measured income flows. Because all individuals above a certain income threshold must file a return, tax returns are particularly well-suited to the study of the upper-end of the income distribution. These are advantages over survey data, which often suffer from small-sample biases or sampling errors (Webber, Tonkin and Shine (forthcoming[14]), Kennedy (2019[15])).

That being said, there are also a number of limitations with tax microdata which should be taken into consideration. The fact that the tax forms are self-assessed implies that there may be underreporting or no disclosure of income flows at all, especially if the likelihood of being audited by tax authorities is low. More importantly, tax microdata only cover forms of income that are useful for tax collection and deduction purposes, which implies that other forms of non-taxable income are not reported in these data. The different datasets used in this report are explored in more detail below.

Personal income tax data

The analysis relies on personal income tax data from the SARS-NT panel which has been compiled by Ebrahim and Axelson (2019[16]). The panel combines for the first time ITR12 and IRP5 tax records and thus provides a comprehensive picture of the taxable income distribution of taxpayers in the formal sector in South Africa. Disentangling tax records by source codes and the number of tax filers per year, the panel also contains, for instance, detailed income information on retirees receiving only income from pension funds and individuals who are self-employed and only submit ITR12 returns. More information on South Africa's tax system can be found in Chapter 4.

Important for the purpose of this report is the availability of ITR12 data on foreign capital income by the source of the income. Disaggregation by source code allows the examination of income streams from interest, dividends or capital gains stemming from capital invested abroad and at home. The original dataset prepared by Ebrahim and Axelson (2019[16]) which covers tax years from 2011 to 2017, has been updated to tax year 2019.[4] SARS has also provided detailed income tax data covering all taxpayers with an ITR12 report for the years 2017 to 2019.

Data from the Voluntary Disclosure and the Special Voluntary Disclosure Programmes

The anonymised VDP dataset provides a detailed overview of applications collected by SARS. The information gathered through the VDP application form discloses the exact date and time of applications for the period from 2017 to early 2020. The dataset encompasses a total of 4287 unique applications with some taxpayers having applied several times. Amounts of previously unpaid taxes disclosed during the submissions are not provided.

The data reports whether the applying entity is an individual or an organisation. By means of an indicator variable the submissions to the VDP are broken down by tax type – whether the application refers to unpaid excise duties, customs duties, personal income taxes, VAT, other income taxes or any other taxes. The data further includes whether applicants submitted anonymously to obtain an indication of the possible relief that may be granted. On this basis, SARS issues a non-binding VDP ruling indicating whether or not, and to what extent, the applicant would qualify for relief. Taxpayers also need to report any years of tax default in the past for which they seek relief through the VDP. This information may provide important insights into patterns of tax evasion over time.

The anonymised SVDP dataset provides an even more comprehensive account of all individual applications to the SVDP programme throughout its active period from 31 October 2016 to 31 August 2017. The information contained in the dataset stems from the SVDP application form that was provided to potential applicants by SARS and SARB through their website. Most of the following information was self-declared by applying taxpayers. The total number of individual SVDP applications is 3123. The total number of successful applications providing entries to most data fields, however, reduces to 375, which is mainly due to incomplete applications that could not be processed by the relevant authorities or were rejected because of ongoing investigations. More specifically, the dataset contains precise information on the date and time of the application to the SVDP and the declared total amount of assets abroad in the respective denominated currency. It further provides information on the corresponding fines applied by SARB in contravention of exchange control regulation relative to the declared amount of assets in both ZAR and original currency.

Moreover, the data shows several geographic indications relating to the "Statement of unauthorised foreign assets and structures as at 29 February 2016", the deadline for filing tax returns for the 2016 tax year. The data discloses foreign locations of non-resident discretionary trusts, their place of effective management, the potential location of investments in other listed financial instruments as well as the locations of bank accounts for short-term deposits. In addition, three indicator variables declare the type of applicant (individual or company), whether the declared assets are vested,[5] and indicate whether the applicant is a holder of a non-resident discretionary trust.

Data exchanged under the Common Reporting Standard

National Treasury has also access to aggregated financial account data received by foreign jurisdictions under the CRS.[6] Exchanged several times during 2017 and 2019, the data provides unique evidence of financial accounts held by South African taxpayers abroad. Apart from the total amount of assets invested in these accounts, the dataset also contains information on the jurisdiction of account incorporation, the different account types such as bank deposits or investment accounts, and payments into these accounts per transmission period. A more detailed description of this dataset is provided in Chapter 6, followed by an in-depth analysis of the information available.

As has been shown, the different datasets used in the study do not only vary in terms of the taxpayer information included but also in their structure such as sample length and frequency of observations. For instance, while individual applications to the VDPs are registered on a daily basis, observations from the SARS-NT panel are included annually, aggregated per taxable income decile. In contrast, due to a different data-generating processes, data from the CRS, the VDPs and income tax returns can be matched per individual and by fiscal year if a corresponding taxpayer appears in all datasets. These characteristics limits the extent to which different data sources can be combined for analytical purposes. Any combined analysis of different datasets in the following sections will thus be clearly stated.

Methodology

This section assesses the responsiveness of taxpayers to various tax transparency initiatives over time through local and foreign capital income tax data. Participation in the VDP and the SVDP as well as the income and wealth structure of their applicants are discussed separately in a subsequent step. The analysis of CRS data as well as the methodology applied will be provided in Chapter 6.

Taxpayer behaviour around implementation dates of tax transparency initiatives can serve as a test of their effectiveness and may provide an indication of prior misconduct. The analysis of taxpayer responsiveness to policies in individual jurisdictions has increasingly been used to assess the impact on tax evasion of both domestic policies (Londoño-Vélez and Ávila-Mahecha (2021[1]); Johannesen et al. (2020[4]); Leenders et al. (2020[3])) as well as international initiatives (Johannesen, 2014[17]). Studies usually rely on variants of a difference-in-differences framework, where a treatment group with exposure to the implementation of a certain policy is compared with a control group whose members are unaffected by the same policy.

In the South African context, detailed aggregated annual data from the SARS-NT panel provide a basis for such an analysis in a more descriptive way. Relying on individual tax returns, total filings by local and foreign capital income derived from interest, dividends or capital gains are compared over time as a first step. In a second step, the trajectories of new tax filings on foreign capital income sources are compared with new domestic filings. Such comparisons can shed light on the perceived increases in detection risk for taxpayers by the implemented policies and may provide a first indication of the impacts of tax transparency in South Africa.

Evidence on tax compliance from tax returns data

The total number of taxpayers reporting foreign interest income peaks in 2014 (Figure 5.1.). During the period from 2011 to 2018, total foreign interest filings are relatively stable at around 10 000 individuals per year in 2011 but started to sharply increase between 2012 and 2014. Foreign interest filings reached a high in 2014 with over 110 000 tax returns, an eleven-fold increase compared to previous years. Individual returns, however, declined relatively quickly thereafter and further flattened until 2019, offsetting the previous sudden surge. Foreign interest however stabilised at a higher level than before the implementation of AEOI at around 20 000 individuals per year. This development is contrasted with local interest income filings. There, tax returns were relatively stable over the period from 2014 to 2016, strongly increased in 2017 and declined again somewhat afterwards.

Figure 5.1. The number of individuals reporting foreign interest income peaks in 2014

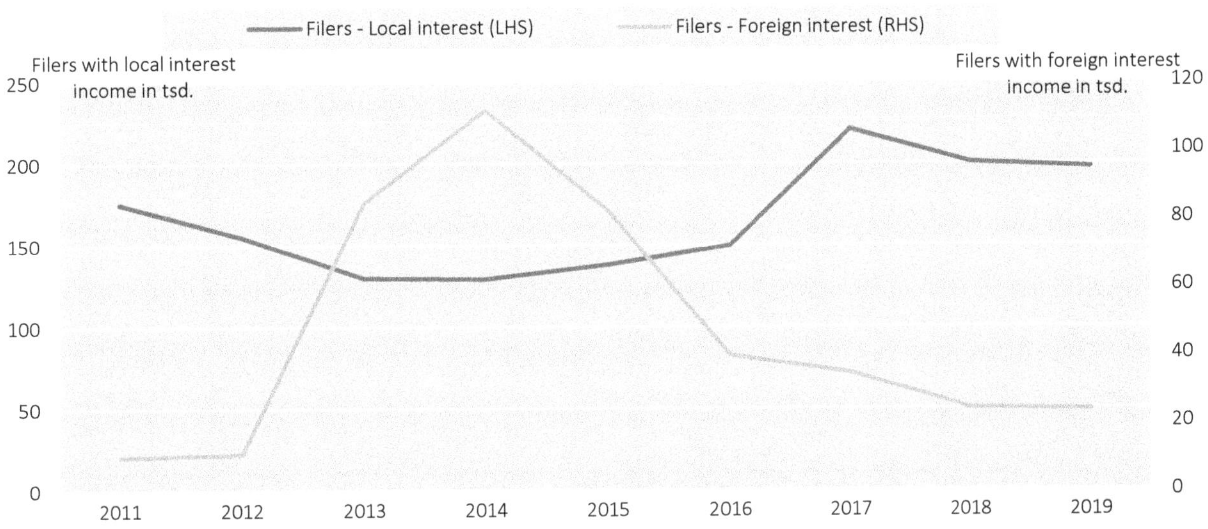

Note: This figure shows the total number of submitted tax reports per year referring to income derived from local interest (source code 4201 in the South African tax code) and foreign interest (source code 4218 in the South African tax code). The tax year usually runs from 1 March to end of February the following year.
Source: OECD calculations based on updated SARS-NT Panel data (Ebrahim and Axelson, 2019[16]).

StatLink https://stat.link/iqedhf

Both peaks in the contrasting trajectories occur around the implementation of major tax transparency initiatives. The fact that in 2014 foreign interest declarations surged while local interest declarations bottomed out suggests higher detection risk for tax evaders with offshore bank accounts following South Africa's public commitment to AEOI and the entry into force of the MAAC in March 2014, as well as the expansion of South Africa's EOIR network prior to that (see Figure 4.3). This may hold, in particular, given the ability through EOI for SARS to obtain information on capital income from assets abroad. From the mid-1990s onwards, the number of overall bilateral EOI agreements entering into force increased steadily, climbing from only a handful in 1995 to over 60 by the time of the global financial crisis. The following decade saw another surge in agreements due to the MAAC and the growth in bilateral agreements. In contrast, agreements entering into force with IFCs started to increase slower and took off later, with the largest increase happening between 2012 and 2015. The fact that the sharp increase in foreign interest filings from 2012 to 2014 could suggest the EOI relationships with IFCs (not EOI relationships overall) are key drivers of increased taxpayer reporting. These effects may have been further compounded by a general tightening of domestic tax enforcement in 2016 through, for instance, the introduction of the SVDP in addition to the already existing VDP. This environment of increasing tax transparency may have therefore induced more taxpayers with income from local interest to submit their tax returns.

Total tax returns for taxable local and foreign dividend income mirror the trajectories of interest income returns. The number of returns for foreign dividends increased seven-fold from 2012 to 2013, surging from 2 170 to 32 555 (Figure 5.2). Subsequently, returns continued to increase slightly in 2014 and broadly decline afterwards. In contrast, returns on taxable local dividends experienced a three-fold increase between 2015 and 2017 and largely remained at that elevated level in the following years. These data also suggest a sharp increase in reported foreign wealth during the years of significantly expanded tax transparency. As is the case with respect to interest income, the increase in domestic capital income and the corresponding decline in foreign source income could suggest repatriation of some assets.

Figure 5.2. The number of individuals reporting foreign dividends income peaks in 2014

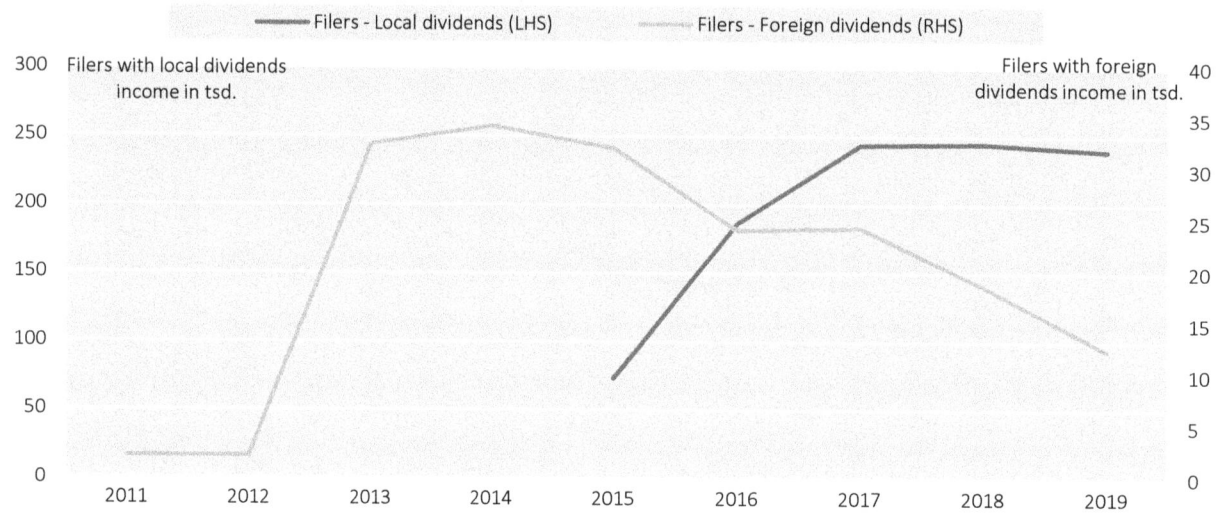

Note: This figure shows the total number of submitted tax reports per year referring to income derived from taxable local dividends (source code 4238 in the South African tax code) and foreign dividends (source code 4216 in the South African tax code). A domestic dividends tax was only introduced in 2014 and therefore data for the source code on taxable local dividends is only available from 2015 onwards. The tax year usually runs from 1 March to end of February the following year.
Source: OECD calculations based on updated SARS-NT Panel data (Ebrahim and Axelson, 2019[16]).

StatLink https://stat.link/mdkg12

Figure 5.3. The number of individuals reporting foreign capital gains increases over time

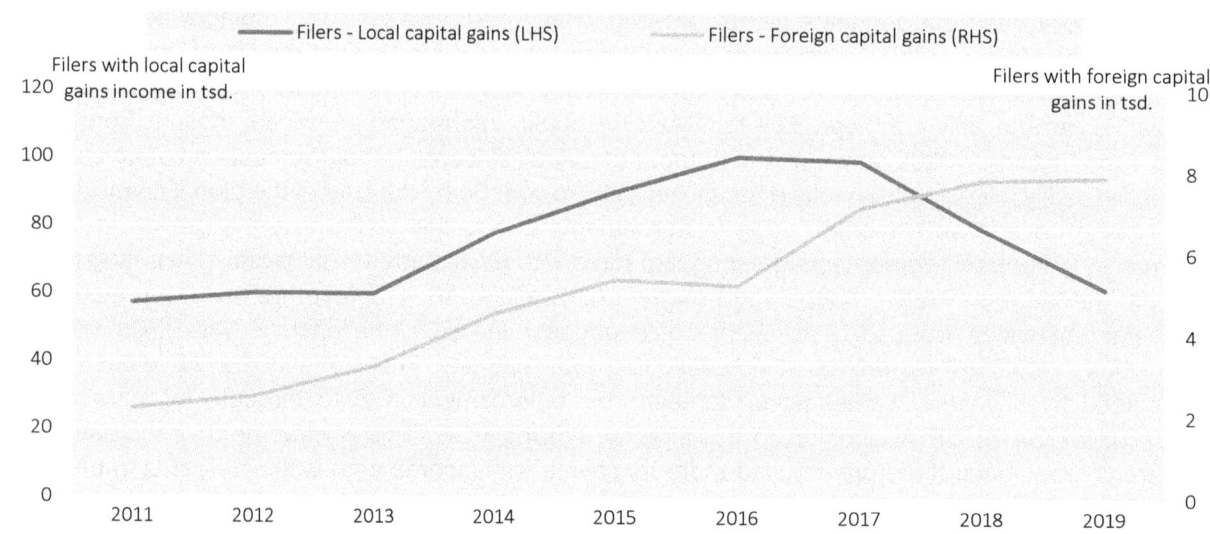

Note: This figure shows the total number of submitted tax reports per year referring to income derived from local capital gains (source code 4250 in the South African tax code) and foreign capital gains (source code 4252 in the South African tax code). The tax year usually runs from 1 March to end of February the following year.
Source: OECD calculations based on updated SARS-NT Panel data (Ebrahim and Axelson, 2019[16]).

StatLink https://stat.link/c7vhsw

In contrast to interest and dividend incomes, total submissions for local and foreign capital gains exhibit a broadly increasing trend without the same sharp peaks over the 2012-2014 period (Figure 5.3). While the numbers of tax returns for local capital gains rose from 2013 onwards and declined after their peak in 2017, returns on foreign capital gains increased until 2015 and continued in 2017. The absence of a sharp increase for capital gains from 2012 to 2014, in contrast to the increase in interest and dividends, aligns with the fact that the expansion of tax transparency was principally over assets that earned interest and dividends (e.g. bank accounts) as opposed to assets that would earn capital gains (e.g. property). The more modest increase could also be a function of the fact that realisations of foreign assets may be more intermittent relative to payments of interest and dividends which are typically annual income.

Figure 5.4. New tax reports for foreign incomes spike in 2014 and 2017

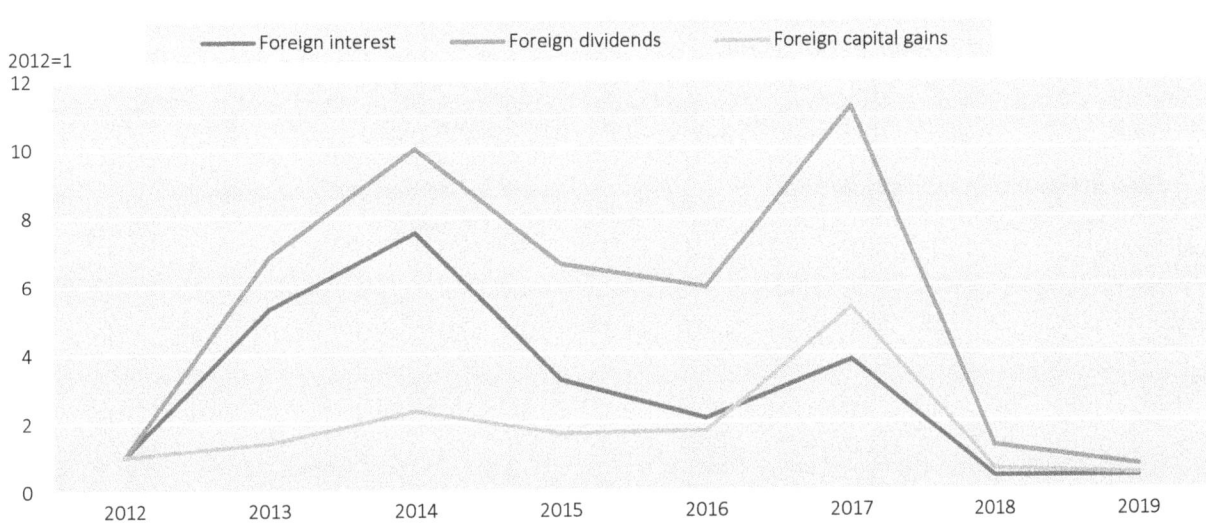

Note: All three series of new filers for foreign income streams are normalised to the base year 2012 (i.e. 2012=1). An increase of 1 in 2013 thus represents an increase of 100% relative to the number of new filers in 2012. The tax year usually runs from 1 March to end of February the following year.
Source: OECD calculations based on updated SARS-NT Panel data (Ebrahim and Axelson, 2019[16]).

StatLink https://stat.link/z8liuc

Another important indication of taxpayer behaviour amid increasing tax transparency are new filings of tax returns per year relative to previous years. Normalised with respect to the tax year 2012, Figure 5.4 shows a dual-hump-shaped trajectory of new tax return filings, i.e. tax return from taxpayers previously unknown to tax authorities, for foreign interest, dividends and capital gains. New reports on all three capital income sources started to increase after 2012 and reached a first peak in 2014. New filings of foreign dividends and interest increased six and nine-fold respectively relative to the base year. In contrast, new tax returns on foreign capital gains only increased slightly during this period. Thereafter, all three foreign income categories experienced a decline in new tax filings. These spikes are consistent with the spikes observed in the amounts disclosed in Figures 5.1, 5.2 and 5.3, and suggest taxpayer responses to South Africa's signature of the MAAC and commitment to exchange information automatically in 2014.

New foreign capital income reports spiked again in 2017. The number of new tax reports surged again in 2017, particularly for foreign capital gains and dividends. Relative to 2016, both income categories experienced a strong increase in new tax filings of over 150% and 80% respectively. This spike in 2017 can likely be attributed to the commencement of AEOI exchanges that year. Foreign interest filings, however, increased comparatively less. While both temporary surges around 2014 and 2017 indicate a responsiveness to South Africa's initial public commitment to AEOI and the later commencement of active exchange, a differential effect over time and between income categories is discernible.

Disclosed amounts of aggregated foreign income by new tax filers suggest that the very top income receivers have tended to disclose more foreign income just before AEOI commencement. There were sharp increases in foreign income by new filers of all income levels as of 2014 followed by a sharp peak in amounts disclosed in 2017 (Figure 5.5, Panel B). The increase in declared foreign income in 2017 relative to previous years also rose with taxable income earned, particularly for the top income receivers. In contrast, foreign incomes disclosed by taxpayers with a history of submitting tax returns experienced a constant increase in revealed amounts (Panel A). Submitted amounts temporarily peak in 2015, drop in 2016 and continue to increase up until 2018. Relative to new filers, the amounts disclosed exhibit a more synchronised pattern across all income distribution fractiles. Significantly, more revenue gains were experienced by existing filers relative to new filers. This suggests that existing filers regularised their tax affairs when South Africa joined the MAAC and committed to AEOI, while a smaller group of new filers only came forward when AEOI commenced.

Figure 5.5. Total foreign income reporting is different for old and new tax return filers

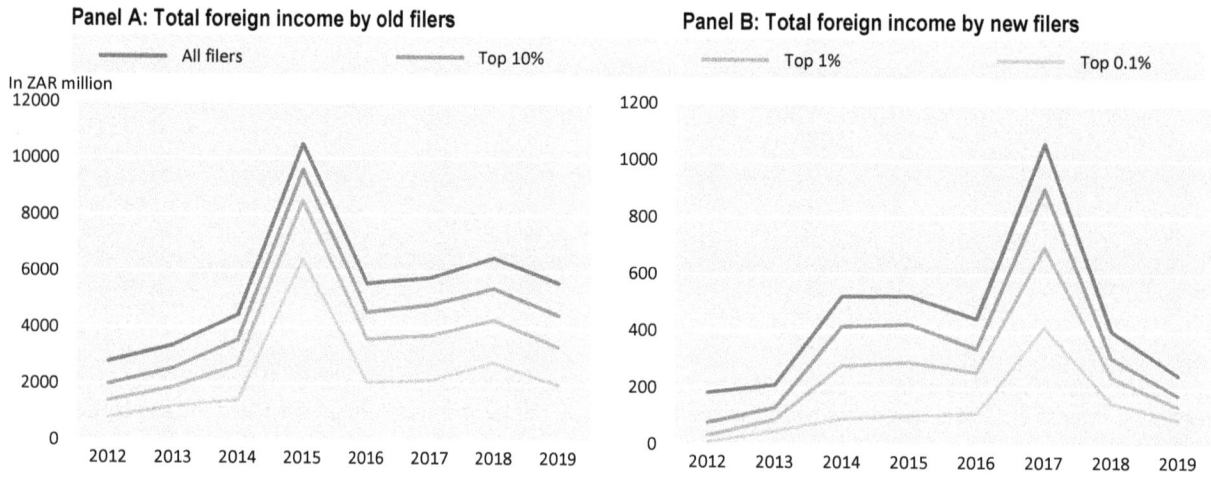

Note: Foreign income aggregates all tax returns submitted in relation to source codes connected to foreign income streams. Old filers refer to taxpayers having filed tax returns in the past relative to the respective year in the sample for a given foreign income source code. New filers refer to taxpayers who have filed for the first time in the respective year relative to previous years in the sample. Old and new tax return filers either shown in their entirety or fractiles are expressed relative to their position in the taxable income distribution.
Source: OECD calculations based on updated SARS-NT Panel data (Ebrahim and Axelson, 2019[16]).

StatLink https://stat.link/d3iegp

A similar pattern can be observed when only inspecting declared foreign capital income by new tax filers. While foreign capital income disclosed by old filers increased constantly over time, reported income by new filers spiked in 2017 (Figure 5.6, Panel B). The declared amount by the top 0.1% of income receivers in 2017 relative to 2016 was disproportionately high compared to lower percentiles. Whereas the increase for all new filers in income declared was about 25-fold relative to the previous year, the top 0.1% disclosed an overall amount close to a 100-times more. The declared share of foreign capital income in total declared income for 2017 was also higher for the very top income earners relative to the remaining segments of the income distribution. These observations provide strong evidence of a sizeable increase in the behavioural responses of the very top income receivers to the increased detection risk associated with the commencement of AEOI, particularly in relation to foreign capital income.

Figure 5.6. Reporting with respect to foreign capital income also shows a distinct pattern for new filers

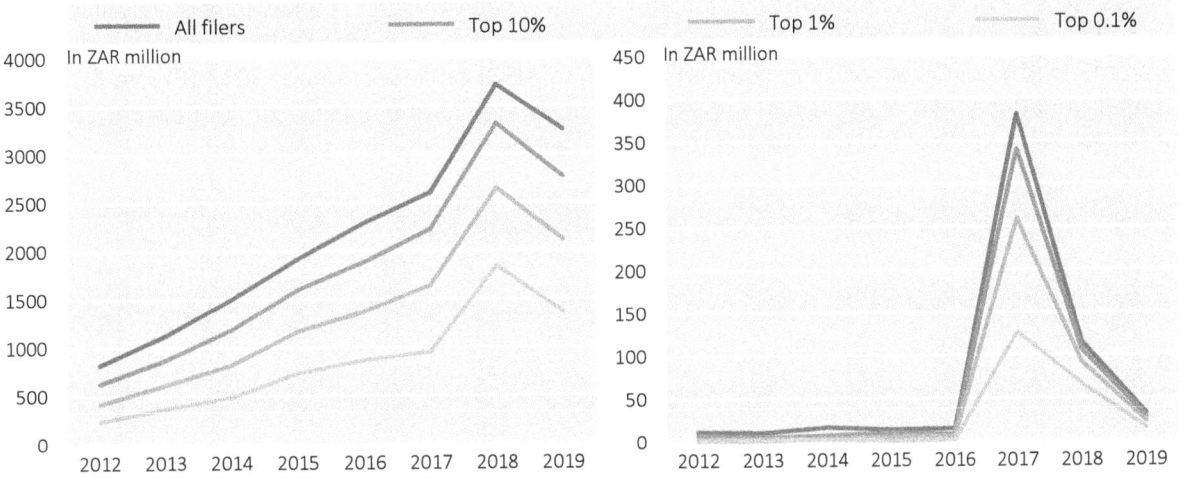

Note: Foreign capital income aggregates all tax returns submitted in relation to source codes connected to foreign capital income streams. Old filers refer to taxpayers having filed tax returns in the past relative to the respective year in the sample for a given foreign capital income source code. New filers refer to taxpayers who have filed for the first time in the respective year relative to previous years in the sample. Old and new tax return files are either shown in their entirety or fractiles are expressed relative to their position in the taxable income distribution.
Source: OECD calculations based on updated SARS-NT Panel data (Ebrahim and Axelson, 2019[16]).

StatLink https://stat.link/vfekxw

Old and new filers of foreign income not only exhibit differences in disclosed amounts but also seem to respond differently to tax transparency standards. Foreign incomes by new filers appear less linear but more responsive to AEOI commencement, while existing taxpayers appear more responsive to EOIR or to AEOI announcement. This may be because EOIR requires the tax authority to have knowledge of a taxpayer to gain access to additional data, and so those taxpayers most at risk from EOIR (where the network expanded sharply between 2012 and 2015) would be taxpayers already known to SARS. AEOI, by contrast, represented a new risk to taxpayers who may not have ever declared foreign income at all, which is consistent with the spike observed. These findings highlight the complementarity of EOIR and AEOI as enforcement tools in South Africa.

Taxpayer responsiveness to domestic tax transparency initiatives

While the previous data series have shown results from aggregated capital income tax returns, data from applications to both VDP and SVDP provide a more direct and more granular snapshot into tax evasion behaviour. Although self-declared and thus carrying certain risks in terms of accuracy, this data provides direct insights into the amounts of previously undeclared assets held abroad and capital incomes received from these sources. The following analyses SVDP and VDP applications by individual programme and examines taxpayer behaviour and income characteristics of those taxpayers that were discovered evading taxes through their participation in the programmes.

Evidence from the SVDP

During the active application window from 1 October 2016 to 31 August 2017, a total of 3123 taxpayers submitted an application to the SVDP. Eventually 375 successful applicants disclosed offshore assets.[7] While throughout most of the application window taxpayers showed relatively little interest in the SVDP, the number of applications rose quickly in late July and peaked just before the end of the programme which coincided with the commencement of AEOI on 1 September 2017 (Figure 5.7). Given the earlier announcement of the SVDP implementation by the finance minister on 24 February 2016, the strong increase in applications this late in the process seems nonetheless surprising.

Figure 5.7. SVDP applications peak before AEOI commencement

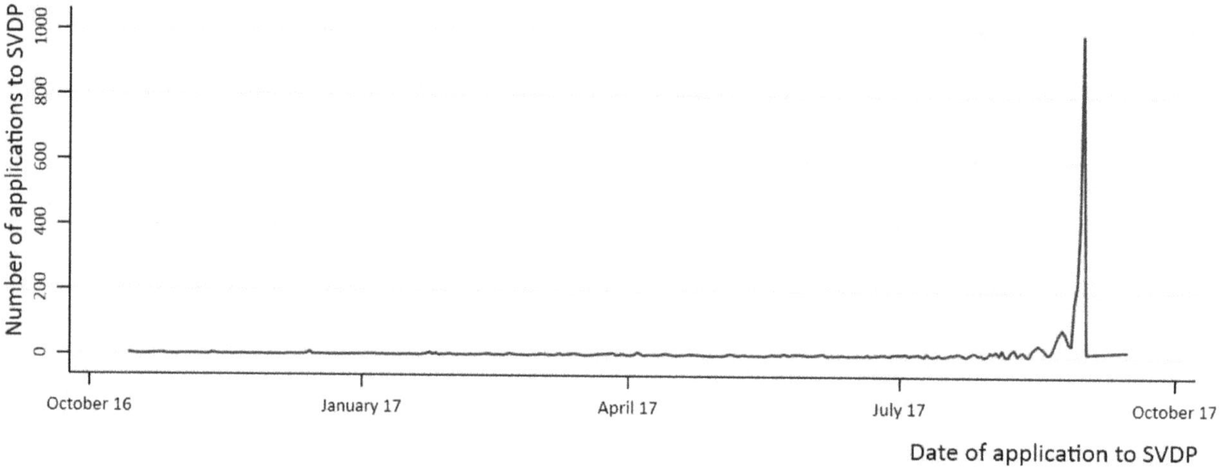

Note: The line presents the number of applications to the SVDP per day.
Source: OECD calculations based on SARS data.

This pattern observed in the South African data of surging applications towards the end of a VDP period follows patterns in other countries. Similar taxpayer behaviour, for instance, has also been reported for US programmes (Langenmayr, 2017[18]). Counterintuitively, suggestive evidence further hints at a potential increase in tax evasion through VDPs on the basis of expected leniency from tax authorities in the future. The long-standing existence of the permanent VDP in South Africa might reinforce such expectations by taxpayers. However, the sudden steep rise in applications despite the pre-existence of the VDP, the early announcement to launch the SVDP and the fact that the programme was explicitly implemented to target offshore wealth prior to AEOI commencement rather indicate a strong behavioural response by taxpayers to an increasing detection risk.

South African taxpayers reported a total of about USD 349 million (ZAR 4.6 billion) of previously undisclosed offshore wealth in the SVDP. The disclosures resulted in close to USD 30 million (ZAR 398.3 million) of additional tax revenues collected by the government through levied fines and taxes (Table 4.1.).[8] This amount roughly equals 60% of the 2017 increase in declared total foreign capital income, relative to 2016, by all old and new tax filers in the previous section (Figure 5.6). The remaining ZAR 282 million or 40% of that increase could be considered as soft disclosures encouraged by overall tightening of tax transparency.

When only accounting for undeclared foreign wealth held in IFCs, the overall amount only reduces to close to USD 300 million (ZAR 3.9 billion), which suggests that South African tax evaders predominantly held undisclosed wealth in IFC jurisdictions.[9] Levies applied to disclosures in the SVDP suggest that less than half of all offshore wealth was repatriated during the settlement process. However, offshore wealth disclosed in the SVDP falls short of amounts uncovered elsewhere. While similar programmes in the United States and Colombia revealed hidden wealth worth about 0.7% and 1.73% of national GDP respectively (Johannesen et al., 2020[4]); (Londoño-Vélez and Ávila-Mahecha, 2021[1]), South Africans only reported about 0.1% of GDP in 2017. This may suggest that South Africans held less non-compliant wealth offshore before the introduction of tax enforcement schemes, or it may suggest an expectation of reduced effectiveness of the schemes relative to other countries.

Table 5.1. Hidden offshore wealth declared in the SVDP

	Number of successful applications	Total amounts disclosed	Additional revenues collected
Across all asset locations	375	USD 348.82 million	USD 29.89 million
Across IFCs only	238	USD 298.96 million	USD 25.71 million

Note: Where denominated in another currency than USD, amounts have been converted to USD by the average annual exchange rate in 2017 (OECD, 2022[19]). The list of IFCs is taken from O'Reilly, Parra Ramirez and Stemmer (2019[20]).
Source: OECD calculations based on SARS data.

Considering only declared non-compliant offshore wealth suggests that the SVDP applicants are largely drawn from the wealthiest individuals in South Africa. As derived from Table 5.1, the average user of offshore accounts reports around USD 930 000 (ZAR 12.4 million) of net wealth abroad and the amount rises to about USD 1.2 million (ZAR 16 million) if only IFCs as account holding jurisdictions are considered. According to recently estimated wealth distribution data for 2017 from Chatterjee et al. (2020[11]), these offshore amounts alone place the average SVDP applicant in the top 10% of South Africa's wealth distribution. Relative to the national average, the typical owner of offshore wealth holds more than 18 times abroad of what the average South Africans own in total.

South African taxpayers historically held their previously undisclosed offshore wealth either in foreign trusts, through direct investments in financial assets such as shares or bonds, or as short-term deposits in bank accounts. Seventy-four out of the 375 SVDP applicants invested at least parts of their assets abroad in trusts. Guernsey and Jersey emerge as the predominant jurisdictions for the legal formation of investment trusts, followed by the British Virgin Islands, the Isle of Man and Switzerland. Other IFCs such as Mauritius or Liechtenstein also play an important role (Figure 5.8, Panel A).[10] The established foreign trusts appear to be predominantly managed in the jurisdiction of their legal formation – if the jurisdiction belongs to the list of IFCs. Figure 5.8 (Panel B) shows that most of the foreign investment trusts formed in IFCs such as Guernsey, Jersey, the Isle of Man or Mauritius are also managed in the same jurisdictions. Where trusts are not managed in the same jurisdiction as they are incorporated, Switzerland emerges as the primary provider for wealth management services.

Figure 5.8. Jurisdictions of offshore trusts and their effective management

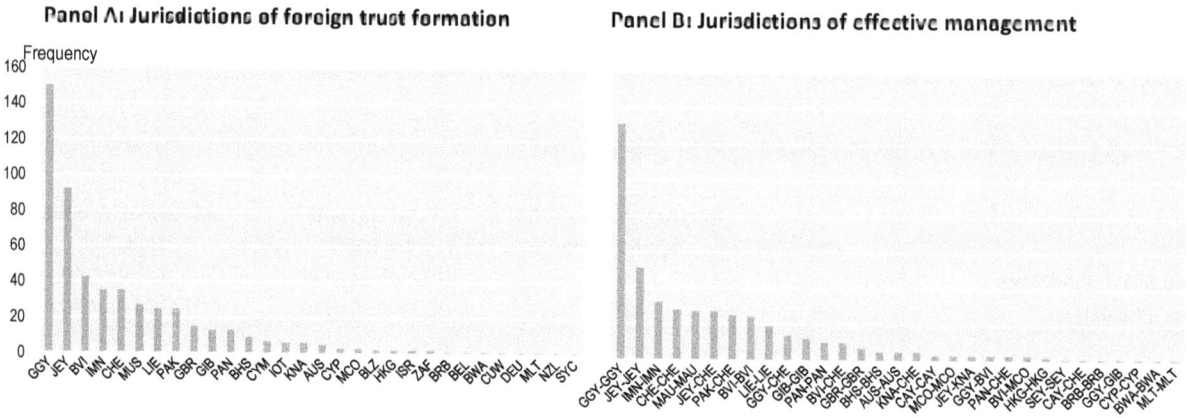

Note: Panel A shows the jurisdictions where foreign trusts were formed per number of appearance in SVDP forms. Panel B combines the jurisdictions of trust formation with their respective jurisdictions of effective trust management as indicated in the SVDP forms.
Source: OECD calculations based on SARS data.

StatLink https://stat.link/9fec6w

Direct investments in financial assets such as stocks and bonds and in rather short-term bank deposits offshore are also predominantly located in IFC jurisdictions (Figure 5.9). In contrast to foreign trusts where the Channel Islands were the dominating jurisdictions, tax-evading South Africans have hidden other investments foremost in accounts in Switzerland or the United Kingdom, followed by Jersey and the Isle of Man. Moreover, two-thirds of all SVDP applicants indicated the use of foreign bank accounts in the form of time and call deposits as part of their evasion strategy, making it the most widespread form of non-compliant investment abroad by frequency (Panel B).[11]

Figure 5.9. Offshore locations of investments in other financial assets

Indicated offshore locations of investments in financial assets and short-term bank deposits

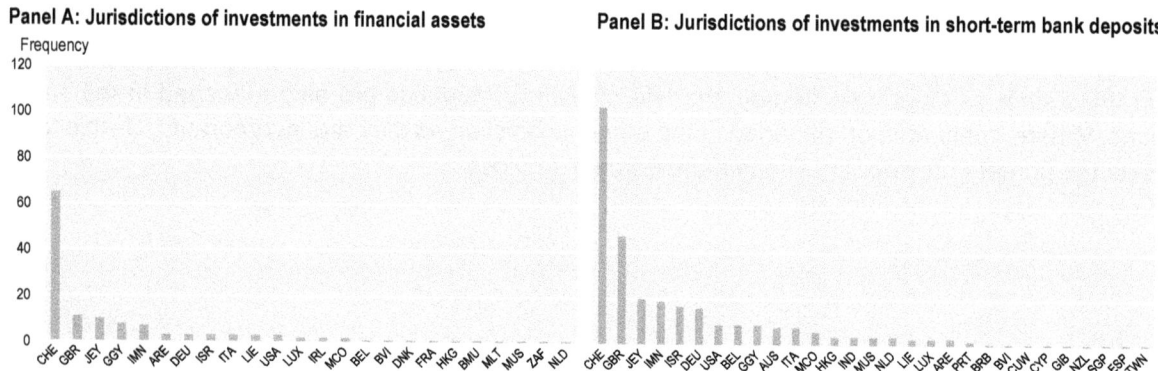

Note: The definition of financial instruments and short-term assets has been taken from the SVDP application form. Financial instruments refer to shares, stocks, bonds and debentured listed on recognised exchanges. Current and other short-term assets refer to bank accounts, call deposits or time deposits.
Source: OECD calculations based on SARS data.

StatLink https://stat.link/p39sta

Disentangling disclosed offshore wealth by location and by average amount per asset class where possible reveals an even more detailed picture of taxpayer behaviour and asset location characteristics.[12] While South Africans within the SVDP appear to have invested their funds across a broad range of jurisdictions, Liechtenstein, Great Britain and Switzerland attract on average the largest total amounts (Figure 5.10). The data suggest that sizeable amounts of capital have flowed into foreign trusts domiciled in Great Britain, followed by Jersey, Guernsey, Monaco, Isle of Man and the Cayman Islands. Switzerland, Great Britain, the United States and Isle of Man receive most of the direct investments in shares or bonds that were tax non-compliant. Investments into short-term assets and deposits in the SVDP are the most wide-spread geographically, led by high average deposits in Liechtenstein, Barbados, but also Italy and to a lower extent Germany and India. Reflecting the previous geographical pattern for the different investments, certain characteristics among jurisdictions arise: SVDP applicants reverted to Great Britain and the Isle of Man for investments in all asset classes. Switzerland and the United States were the dominant location for bank deposits and direct investments into listed assets. IFCs such as Liechtenstein, Barbados, Monaco or Hong Kong attracted on average the largest deposits. These observations further confirm previous findings by, for instance, O'Reilly, Parra Ramirez and Stemmer (2019[20]) and Harrington (2016[6]), who document a division of labour in services provided and a specialisation in business models among IFCs catering to the different needs of customers.

Figure 5.10. Average wealth hidden abroad per jurisdiction and asset class

Average value of assets held abroad per identified asset class

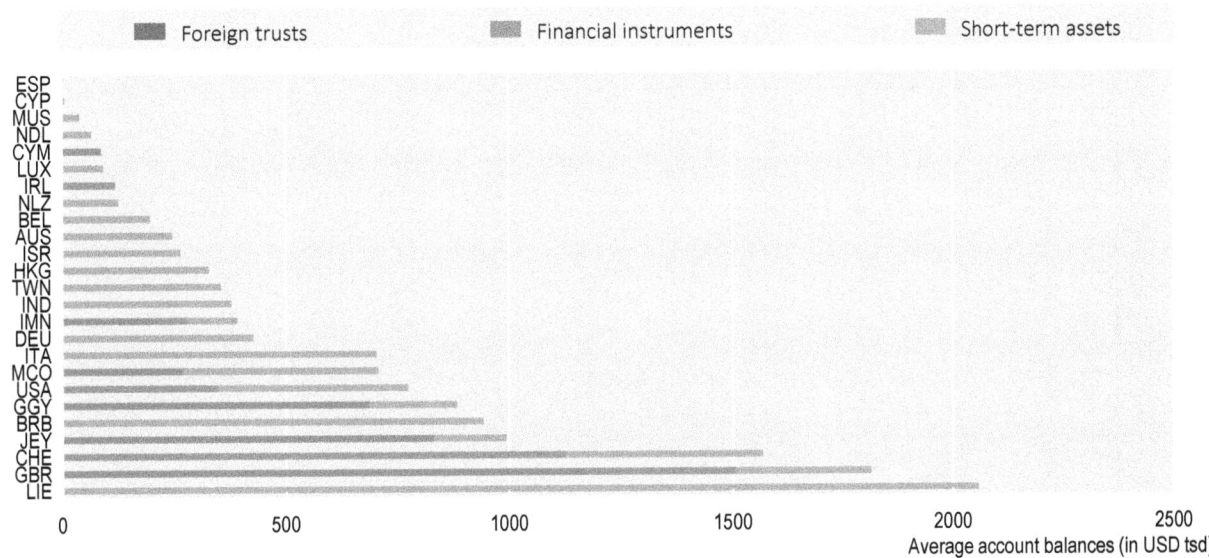

Note: The definition of financial instruments and short-term assets has been taken from the SVDP application form. Financial instruments refer to shares, stocks, bonds and debentures listed on recognised exchanges. Current and other short-term assets refer to bank accounts, call or time deposits.
Source: OECD calculations based on SARS data.

StatLink https://stat.link/91n3ol

EOIR agreements had been in place between South Africa and almost all IFCs listed as foreign investment jurisdictions before the launch of the SVDP. As shown before, the EOIR network has expanded particularly since the global financial crisis. While early agreements with Luxembourg and Switzerland entered respectively into force in September 2000 and January 2009, other relevant jurisdictions such as the Channel Islands followed shortly through the MAAC (OECD (2021[21]), Annex 2). The fact that large swaths of SVDP applications in respect of offshore wealth held in these jurisdictions were submitted as late as August 2017 raises the question of whether expansions in EOIR relationships were, in their own right, an effective deterrent to tax non-compliance, particularly for new tax filers. It may have been the case that tax authorities lacked the capacity or information to take full advantage of new EOIR relationships over this period. By contrast, commitment and commencement of AEOI seemed to exert strong detection pressure on non-compliant taxpayers resulting in a substantial increase in disclosure.[13]

Evidence from the VDP

Like the SVDP, applications by taxpayers to the VDP strongly increased in August 2017 just before the commencement of active information exchange under the CRS in early September 2017. The numbers of submissions remained relatively stable throughout the sample period from March 2016 to November 2020 except for a peak in August 2017 (Figure 5.11). While on average 75 individual applications were submitted per month, the number rose to 348 on 31 August 2017 alone, a total of 948 in that month. After the AEOI commencement applications quickly fell again and remained subdued for the rest of the observation period. This sudden increase in applications prior to active AEOI on 1 September 2017 is suggestive of a large number of taxpayers applying to the VDP in response to an enhanced detection risk, albeit with a rather temporary effect. Similar temporary impacts of tax transparency agreements entering into force on VDPs have also been documented, for instance, by Andersson, Schroyen and Tosvik (2019[22]).

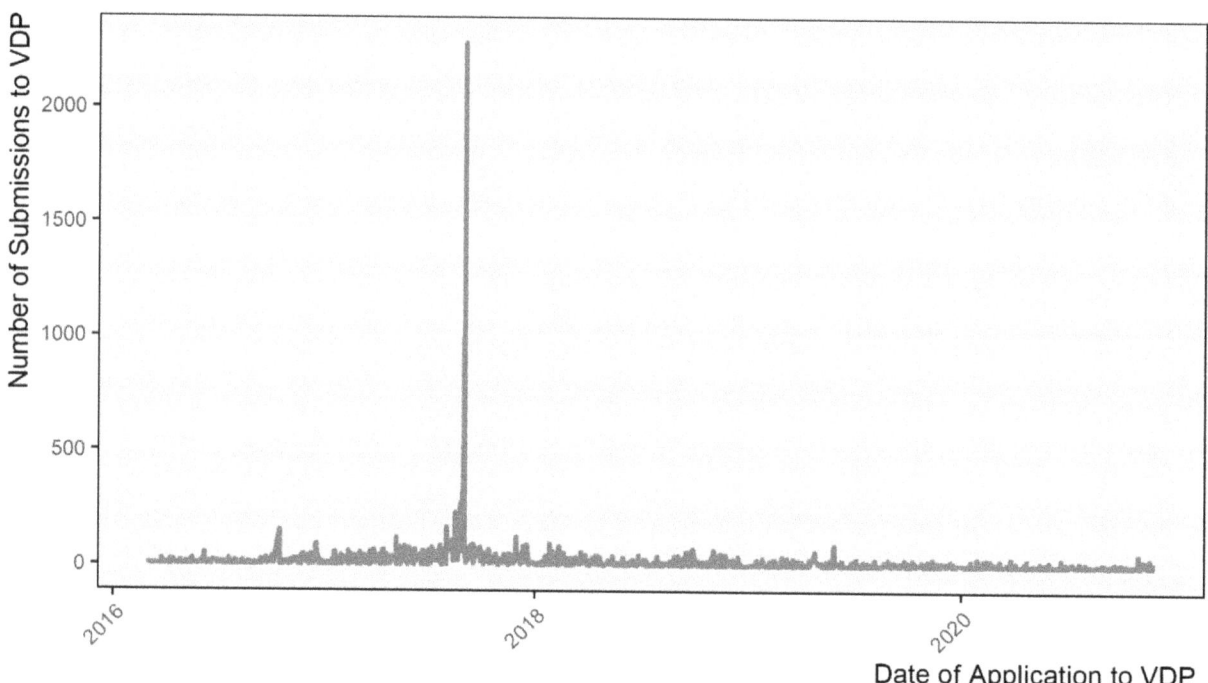

Note: The line presents the number of applications to the VDP per day.
Source: OECD calculations based on SARS data.

The strongest response can be observed for individuals who declared tax liabilities in relation to income taxes. When breaking down applications by tax and entity type in Figure 5.12, the rise in applications among individuals for income taxes (Panel A) reflects the developments previously shown for total applications. With 4271 out of 4287 applications involving income taxes other than salaries, declared tax defaults for income taxes have been the vast majority. A small fraction of taxpayers accumulated tax liabilities across several categories involving apart from income taxes also evasion of VAT, taxes from labour income or other unspecified taxes. Evasion of excise and customs taxes was not reported as neither of those categories were the subject of the VDP. The fact that no spike was observed in VDP applications for any other tax category other than personal income tax suggests that these developments were driven by the increased availability of information arising from the implementation of AEOI.[14]

The effect for organisations and entities has been rather subdued when compared to individuals. While around 2017 a small peak in income tax defaults is discernible for organisations, the scale and length of the surge in applications has been small compared to individuals (Figure 5.12., Panel B). Applications by organisations for other tax categories do not show major changes over time and remain much less frequent across the entire sample period. Despite encouraging voluntary compliance by both individuals and organisations, the VDP has thus shown to be much more attractive for individuals who had previously been evading income taxes.

Figure 5.12. VDP applications by tax type

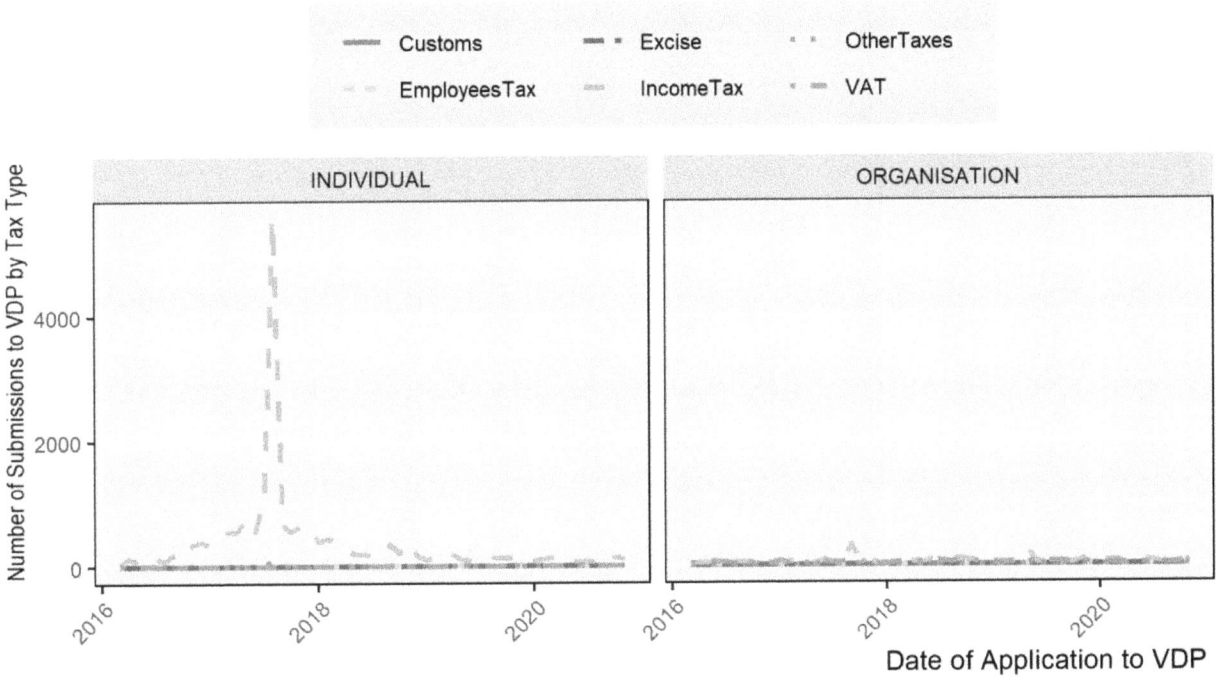

Note: The chart shows the number of VDP applications by tax type over time, divided by individuals or organisations.
Source: OECD calculations based on SARS data.

Of additional interest are the reported years of tax default in the past per VDP application, which in very few cases extend back to 1988. These applications not only precede the official introduction of the programme in 2012 but also its then retroactive eligibility as early as the 2002 tax year. Taxpayers reported on average a period of tax non-compliance for about 5 years with the majority of cases falling into the period from 2007 to 2017. Longer-term evasion on a continuous basis for more than 10 years can be detected for about every fifth applicant. Usually evasive behaviour is just stopped before the application to the programme. The duration of tax evasion revealed through the VDP shows that the notably long duration of non-compliance in many cases suggests that tax evasion is more systematic than a one-off occurrence.

Almost one half of all successful SVDP applicants also participated in the VDP. Compared to VDP-only applicants, these taxpayers exclusively filed for past income tax liabilities from other income than labour in the VDP. The same taxpayers disclosed on average more than double the amount of offshore assets under the SVDP compared to SVDP-only participants. While programme participants may have simultaneously evaded several taxes, this observation lends further confidence to a statement by SARS officials about the strong relation between VDP applications and undeclared foreign income (AU/ATAF/OECD, 2020[23]). Moreover, applicants to both programmes evaded their income taxes over multiple years as Figure 5.13 shows. While there is some evidence that larger offshore wealth implies longer periods of evasion, taxpayers having participated in both programmes declared on average non-compliance for about 8 years on average, more than 2 years on average longer than VDP-only applicants. The disclosures of more than 40% of these taxpayers evidence non-compliance over a period longer than a decade, sometimes documenting evasion as early as 1998.

Figure 5.13. Tax evasion over time by dual SVDP-VDP applicants

Years of undeclared income by applicants to both SVDP and VDP programmes

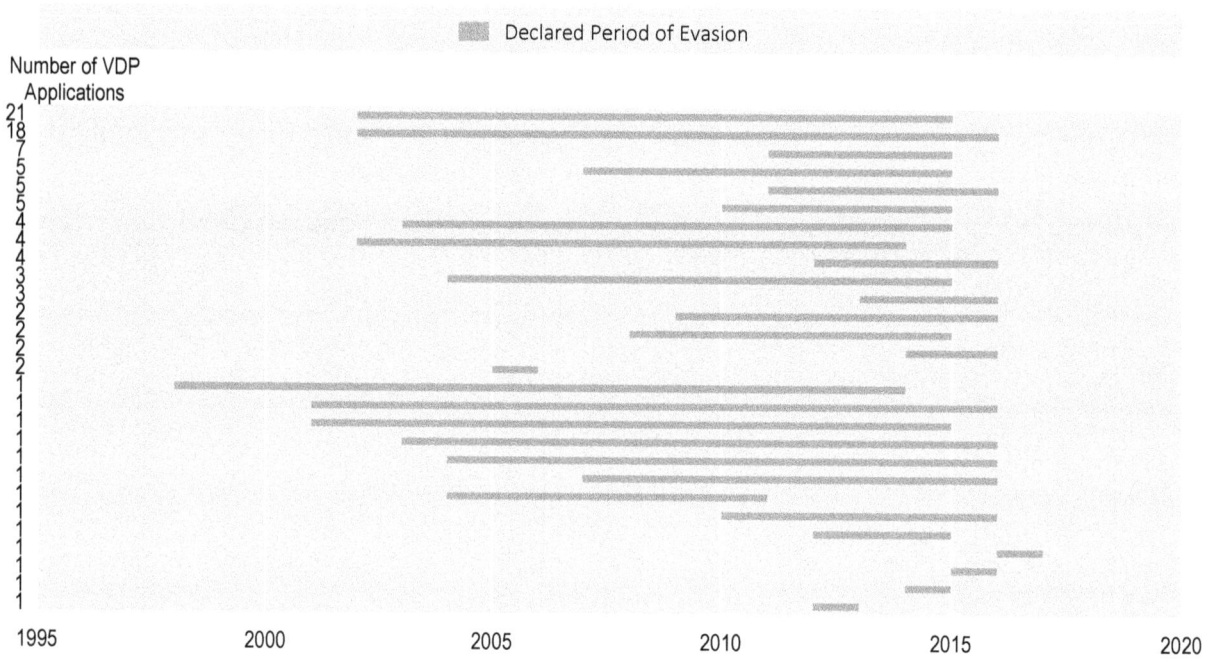

Note: The figure presents the declared duration of evasion of dual VDP – SVDP applicants over time, ranging from 1998 to 2017. Out of the total 144 SVDP participants who also applied to the VDP, 100 applicants declared evasion continuously for more than one year. 44 applicants not shown only declared one missing year or single years across the entire period.
Source: OECD calculations based on SARS data.

StatLink https://stat.link/v4k791

Overall the analysis above suggests that tax evasion has been a long-standing phenomenon for some taxpayers. South Africa's participation in multilateral initiatives to increase global tax transparency such as the AEOI, however, appear to have positively impacted taxpayer compliance. Amid this heightened risk of detection, the VDP and the SVDP in particular have managed to encourage taxpayers with a longer history of tax non-compliance and with relatively large amounts of offshore assets to come forward. Both global and domestic initiatives can thus be considered important elements of South Africa's fight against tax evasion and IFFs. This also implies that in order to accumulate even partially revealed offshore amounts in the past, capital must have illicitly flown out of the country for quite some time.

Characterising SVDP/VDP applicants

The amount of offshore assets declared in the SVDP is a key source of data on previously hidden wealth and the extent of IFFs pre-dating this period. While the overall amount of around USD 349 million that has been revealed by 375 applicants during the active period of the programme is in itself a success, these numbers need nonetheless be set into context relative to the entire population of taxpayers. Linking SVDP and VDP with income tax data thus allows for an assessment of whether the characteristics of SVDP and VDP applicants are representative of the entire sample of taxpayers in terms of income structure and the respective asset amounts hidden abroad.

Figure 5.14. The top income levels hold a majority share of total SVDP offshore wealth

Share of offshore wealth per percentile of taxable income in total offshore wealth declared in the SVDP

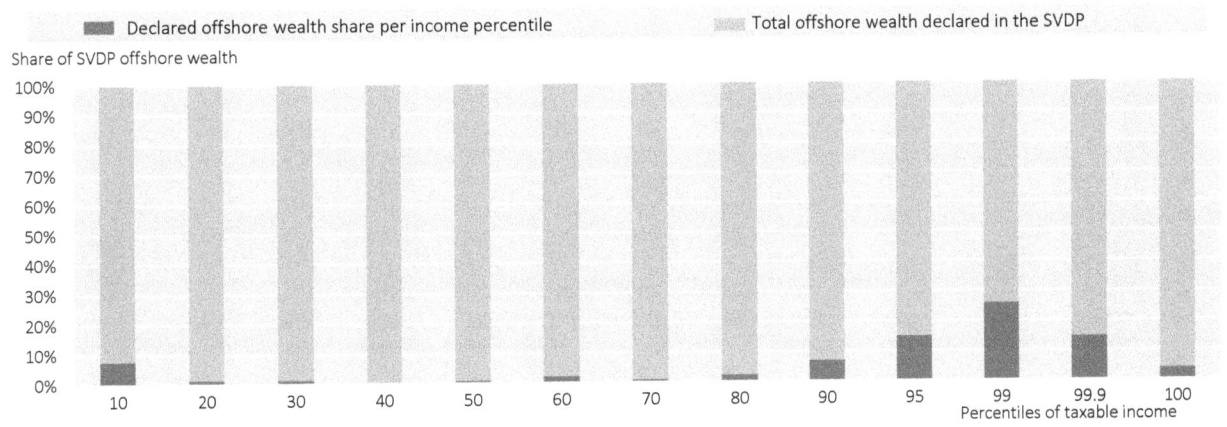

Source: OECD calculations based on SARS data.

StatLink https://stat.link/jb5czw

The top percentiles in taxable income represent the largest share in total offshore wealth declared in the SVDP (Figure 5.14). In line with expectations and the evidence from related literature on South Africa and other countries (e.g. Orthofer, (2016[13]); Londoño-Velèz and Ávila-Mahecha, (2021[1])), shares of total SVDP offshore wealth remain negligible for the lower income deciles, except for the lowest decile, and increase from the 7th decile onwards. The top 0.1% claims a share of about 25% of total declared wealth. Surprisingly, the share of assets held abroad shrinks to 17% for the top 0.01% and to a mere 4% of the total amount declared for the highest income bracket. The respective number of applications per decile mirrors the development in wealth shares. Applications in the lowest percentile were with 32 submissions relatively high, slowly increased to 87 in the 99th percentile and dropped to only 4 applications in the top percentile. These observations raise questions over whether all eligible foreign wealth owners applied and whether some of the wealthiest taxpayers declared less wealth through the SVDP because they remained confident that they would continue to be able to hide their wealth offshore.

SVDP and VDP participants show a distinctive income pattern that contrasts with other taxpayers. While more than 70% of all taxpayers derive their main income from labour, only about 25% of SVDP and VDP applicants do so (Figure 5.15). Income from local capital income such as interest or capital gains provide the main income for about 10% to 13% of programme applicants. A similar share of participating taxpayers can rely on a director's income. Income obtained from retirement funds or pensions, particularly among SVDP participants, may point to a higher age of these taxpayers. Partly in contrast to expectations from programmes implemented elsewhere, foreign capital income as the dominant source of income only plays a marginal role for SVDP and VDP applicants. While around 2% of successful applicants derive most of their income from assets abroad, the general taxpayer population, the non-applicants, seem to rely on other sources. Moreover, most taxpayers participating in either one of the programmes declare only one category of foreign capital income. However, the on average only marginally higher foreign income shares in total taxable income for VDP applicants relative to the general taxpayer population may raise doubts about the validity of VDP declarations, particularly given the steep increase in capital income relative to overall income and wealth levels as documented in Bassier and Woolard (2020[8]) and Chatterjee, Czajka and Gethin (2020[11]).

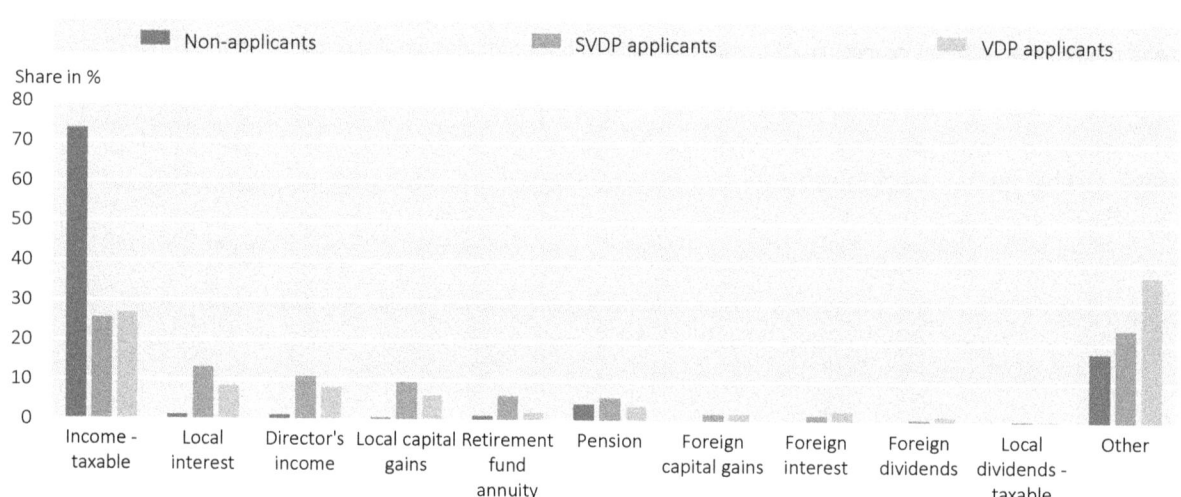

Figure 5.15. Main source of income for SVDP/VDP applicants and non-applicants

Note: The figure compares the main income source per source code of SVDP and VDP applicants to non-applicants for the tax year 2017.
Source: OECD calculations based on SARS data.

StatLink https://stat.link/08qijp

These findings by income category bear nonetheless strong resemblance with results from the amnesty programme in the Netherlands. There, VDP applicants earned significantly more often pension income, income from self-employment and to a lower extent director's income and capital income than the general taxpayer population (Leenders et al., 2020[3]). Most participating taxpayers thus do not seem to derive a significant amount of their income from foreign investments; instead, they seem to have invested substantial shares of their regular taxable income abroad. Similar to the Dutch case, these results may suggest that VDP/SVDP applicants in South Africa do not necessarily belong to the best-off part of society or may have insufficiently declared foreign capital income in the past. Overall these findings signal that the VDP has incentivised individuals with incomes other than labour income – predominantly from foreign capital income - to declare past tax non-compliance. Given the timing of applications, commencement of active information exchange under the CRS appears to have encouraged non-compliant taxpayers to apply to the VDP.

Results and policy implications

This chapter has analysed by means of individual anonymised tax data the responsiveness of South African taxpayers to tax transparency initiatives and dissects the impact of the VDP and the SVDP. Tax evasion is shown to have a long history and has been concentrated among the very wealthy and top income receivers. However, results suggest that taxpayers have responded to tax transparency initiatives, particularly to multilateral ones that increase the global risk of detection. Moreover, domestic transparency initiatives (SVDP/VDP) have been successful in encouraging evaders to come forward, but taxpayer responsiveness appears to have been largely triggered by the commencement of AEOI under the CRS and potentially to the expansion of the EOIR network to several key IFCs. In contrast to bilateral EOIR relationships and corroborating findings about the impact of multilateral tax transparency elsewhere, the commencement of AEOI thus also appears to have strongly supported domestic policy initiatives (Andersson, Schroyen and Tosvik, 2019[22]). This can be seen in the strong taxpayer responses observed immediately before the implementation of AEOI shown above.

Assessed SVDP/VDP applications provide detailed insights into the evasion behaviour of taxpayers, their investment strategies and geographic reach. While evasion by the very top income recipients still appears to exist but is increasingly detected, the analysis also suggests that the VDPs have historically been attractive to individuals with incomes other than labour income and, in particular, those whose incomes are predominantly derived from foreign capital income. Fines charged as a result of application, together with constantly higher tax revenues collected from the top income earners due to strengthened compliance, may lead to a rise in effective tax progressivity as a result of these initiatives. The applications also highlight the relationship between the different IFCs such as their division of labour in services provided or the effective management of investment vehicles. Tax-evading South Africans invested on average the largest sums in bank deposits across a wide range of IFC jurisdictions. Investments in foreign trusts were also popular, with a preference for a small number of IFCs, such as the Channel Islands. Most of these trusts were also managed in the same jurisdiction as they were incorporated.

The implications for tax policy and tax administration are several-fold. Overall, continued use of EOI in South Africa is required. Increasing the more effective use of bilateral EOIR, particularly with well-known IFCs, should be a key priority. As will be discussed below, better domestic enforcement also demands an enhancement of inter-agency collaboration across the different relevant authorities to enable a comprehensive analysis of taxpayer data. The improvement in data access, for instance by pooling available data at one single location, may further help to increase data quality and ensure timely updates. Taken together, these policy initiatives will not only increase the potential for higher levels of revenue collection but may help support a fairer and more progressive tax system for all taxpayers.

References

Advani, A. and A. Summers (2020), "Capital gains and hidden inequality", *Advantage Magazine: Austerity 10th Anniversary Special* Summer, pp. 24-27, https://warwick.ac.uk/fac/soc/economics/research/centres/cage/news/03-06-20-advantage_magazine__summer/article-6/6._capital_gains_and_hidden_inequality.pdf. [9]

Alstadsaeter, A., N. Johannesen and G. Zucman (2019), "Tax Evasion and Inequality", *American Economic Review*, Vol. 109/6, pp. 2073-2103. [2]

Andersson, J., F. Schroyen and G. Tosvik (2019), *The impact of international tax information exchange agreements on the use of tax amnesty: evidence from Norway*, https://papers.ssrn.com/sol3/Delivery.cfm/SSRN_ID3463645_code1391513.pdf?abstractid=3463645&mirid=1. [22]

AU/ATAF/OECD (2020), *Tax Transparency in Africa 2020 - Africa Initiative Progress Report*, OECD Publishing, https://www.oecd.org/tax/transparency/documents/Tax-Transparency-in-Africa-2020.pdf. [23]

Bassier, I. and I. Woolard (2020), *Exclusive growth? Rapidly increasing top incomes amid low amid low national growth in South Africa*, Southern Africa - Towards Inclusive Economic Development (SA-TIED). [8]

Beer, S., M. Coelho and S. Léduc (2019), "Hidden Treasures: The Impact of Automatic Exchange of Information on Cross-Border Tax Evasion", *IMF Working Paper No. 19/286*. [24]

Chatterjee, A., L. Czajka and A. Gethin (2020), "Estimating the distribution of household wealth in South Africa", *UNU-WIDER Working Paper 45*, https://doi.org/10.35188/UNU-WIDER/2020/802-3. [11]

Chetty, R. et al. (eds.) (2021), "Tax Evasion by the Wealthy: Measurement and Implications", *NBER Working Paper No. 28542*, http://www.nber.org/papers/w28542. [5]

Chetty, R. et al. (eds.) (forthcoming), *Using Tax Data to Better Capture Top Incomes in Official UK Income Inequality Statistics*, Chicago University Press. [14]

Ebrahim, A. and C. Axelson (2019), "The creation of an individual level panel using administrative tax microdata in South Africa", *UNU-WIDER Working Paper 661-6*, https://doi.org/10.35188/UNU-WIDER/2019/661-6. [16]

Fagareng, A. et al. (2020), "Heterogeneity and Persistence in Returns to Wealth", *Econometrica*, Vol. 88/1, pp. 115-170, https://doi.org/10.3982/ECTA14835. [10]

Guvenen, F., G. Kaplan and J. Song (2014), "How Risky Are Recessions for Top Earners?", *American Economic Review: Papers & Proceedings*, Vol. 104/5, pp. 148-153, http://dx.doi.org/10.1257/aer.104.5.148. [7]

Harrington, B. (2016), *Capital without Borders: Wealth Managers and the One Percent*, Harvard University Press. [6]

Hundenborn, J., I. Woolard and J. Jellema (2019), "The effect of top incomes on inequality in South Africa", *International Tax and Public Finance*, Vol. 26, pp. 1018-1047, https://doi.org/10.1007/s10797-018-9529-9. [12]

Johannesen, N. (2014), "Tax evasion and Swiss bank deposits", *Journal of Public Economics*, Vol. 111, pp. 46-62, https://doi.org/10.1016/j.jpubeco.2013.12.003. [17]

Johannesen, N. et al. (2020), "Taxing Hidden Wealth: The Consequences of U.S. Enforcement Initiatives on Evasive Foreign Accounts", *American Economic Journal: Economic Policy*, Vol. 12/3, pp. 312-346, https://doi.org/10.1257/pol.20180410. [4]

Kennedy, S. (2019), "The potential of tax microdata for tax policy", *OECD Taxation Working Papers*, No. 45, OECD Publishing, Paris, https://dx.doi.org/10.1787/d2283b8e-en. [15]

Langenmayr, D. (2017), "Voluntary disclosure of evaded taxes — Increasing revenue, or increasing incentives to evade?", *Journal of Public Economics*, Vol. 151, pp. 110-125, https://doi.org/10.1016/j.jpubeco.2015.08.007. [18]

Leenders, W. et al. (2020), "Offshore Tax Evasion and Wealth Inequality: Evidence from a Tax Amnesty in the Netherlands", *EconPol Working Paper 52*, Vol. 4, https://www.ifo.de/DocDL/EconPol_Working_Paper_52_Offshore_Tax_Evasion.pdf. [3]

Londoño-Vélez, J. and J. Ávila-Mahecha (2021), "Enforcing Wealth Taxes in the Developing World: Quasi-Experimental Evidence from Colombia", *American Economic Review: Insights*, Vol. 3/2, pp. 131-148, https://doi.org/10.1257/aeri.20200319. [1]

O'Reilly, P., K. Parra Ramirez and M. Stemmer (2019), "Exchange of information and bank deposits in international financial centres", *OECD Taxation Working Papers*, No. 46, OECD Publishing, Paris, https://dx.doi.org/10.1787/025bfebe-en. [20]

OECD (2022), *Exchange rates* (indicator), https://dx.doi.org/10.1787/037ed317-en (accessed on 22 March 2022). [19]

OECD (2021), *Global Forum on Transparency and Exchange of Information for Tax Purposes: South Africa 2021 (Second Round, Phase 1): Peer Review Report on the Exchange of Information on Request*, Global Forum on Transparency and Exchange of Information for Tax Purposes, OECD Publishing, Paris, https://dx.doi.org/10.1787/fed716dd-en. [21]

Orthofer, A. (2016), "Wealth inequality in South Africa: Evidence from survey and tax data", *REDI3x3 Working Paper 15*, http://redi3x3.org/sites/default/files/Orthofer%202016%20REDI3x3%20Working%20Paper%2015%20-%20Wealth%20inequality.pdf. [13]

Notes

[1] For the purposes of this and the following chapter, the terms 'non-compliant offshore wealth' and 'undeclared foreign wealth' are used interchangeably and are used to describe wealth held in foreign jurisdictions that is associated with tax non-compliance.

[2] The ownership of these assets is generally highly concentrated. The top 10% of the wealth distribution own more than 99% of all bonds and stock held in the economy and in general more than half of all forms of assets, including pension assets, housing wealth or business assets. The top 1% alone holds more than one-tenth of all forms of assets and as much as 90% of bonds and corporate shares (Chatterjee, Czajka and Gethin, 2020[11]).

[3] This data has been provided by SARS to South African National Treasury and analysed jointly with South Africa National Treasury.

[4] More information on the SARS-NT panel can be found in Ebrahim and Axelson (2019[16]).

[5] Rights and interests arising from the legal ownership of the asset that cannot be taken away by any third party such as e.g. retirement plans or insurance contracts.

[6] No data exchanged under the Common Reporting Standard was shared with the OECD in a disaggregated way due to confidentiality standards pertaining to data exchanged under the Common Reporting Standard.

[7] The discrepancy between the total number of applications and successful applications either hails from tax authority investigations against the applicant already underway by the time of submission or incomplete documentation provided by the applying taxpayer.

[8] In this section, USD amounts have been converted to ZAR by the average annual exchange rate in 2017 (OECD, 2022[19]).

[9] O'Reilly, Parra Ramirez and Stemmer (2019) have identified the following list of IFC jurisdictions: Andorra; Anguilla; Antigua and Barbuda; Aruba; Bahamas; Bahrain; Barbados; Belize; Bermuda; British Virgin Islands; Cayman Islands; Cook Islands; Costa Rica; Curacao; Cyprus; Dominica; Gibraltar; Grenada; Guatemala; Guernsey; Hong Kong, China; Isle of Man; Jersey; Lebanon; Liechtenstein; Luxembourg; Macau, China; Malaysia; Malta; Marshall Islands; Mauritius; Monaco; Montserrat; Nauru; Niue; Palau; Panama; Saint Kitts and Nevis; Saint Lucia; Saint Vincent and the Grenadines; American Samoa; San Marino; Seychelles; Singapore; Switzerland; Turks and Caicos Islands; United Arab Emirates; Uruguay; and Vanuatu.

[10] Non-IFC jurisdictions also feature prominently, including jurisdictions which are particular locations for the South African diaspora such as the United Kingdom and Australia.

[11] Other than checking or savings accounts, call and time deposits offer higher interest rates for minimum balance requirements. Time deposits further demand a set period of time with interest rates rising the longer money remains deposited in the account.

[12] SVDP applicants mostly disclosed the total amount of offshore wealth without precise allocation across the different investments. Thus only a fraction of previously undeclared offshore wealth could be uniquely assigned to a single asset class and jurisdiction.

[13] Beer, Coelho and Léduc (2019[24]) and O'Reilly, Parra-Ramirez and Stemmer (2019[20]), for instance, document a generally smaller impact of EOIR on offshore bank deposits relative to AEOI.

[14] The expansion in information was not, for example available for other tax categories such as excises of VAT.

6 Assessing the size of undeclared foreign wealth and IFFs through the CRS

Key messages

- This chapter analyses unique tax data on foreign financial accounts exchanged under the CRS and provides an order-of-magnitude estimate of IFFs in South Africa.
- Accounts in IFCs represent a significant majority of all foreign assets reported through the CRS, but account for less than half of all transmitted accounts.
- South African non-compliant foreign wealth in IFCs is estimated to amount to between USD 40 billion and USD 54 billion in 2018.
- This estimated stock of non-compliant foreign wealth suggests that between USD 3.5 billion and USD 5 billion in IFFs have left South Africa annually over the last decade.
- While important progress has been made, the analysis suggests that matching CRS accounts with domestic tax records continues to be a challenge for South Africa.
- The improvement of analytical capacities in the tax authority to make better use of available financial account information transmitted through the CRS should be a key priority, as should be the increased use of EOIR.
- Enhanced collaboration and augmented data sharing across relevant authorities would further strengthen analytical and enforcement efforts in South Africa.

Introduction

The objective of this chapter is to provide an assessment of the amount of previously undeclared foreign wealth held abroad by South Africans and to derive from it an order-of-magnitude estimate of IFFs in South Africa over recent years. The inability to directly quantify tax evasion, wealth hidden abroad and IFFs demands indirect approaches to estimation. Based on the data sources and the analysis discussed in the previous chapters, this chapter relies on several descriptive and quantitative approaches to estimate the extent of IFFs. Key to this is the use of statistics based on data received by South Africa under the CRS, which provides a first look at the foreign wealth holdings of South Africans, which may not have previously been reported. Given the uniqueness of the CRS data, a short overview of its coverage and the required data cleaning procedure is provided before further analysis of IFFs.[1]

Overview of South African CRS data

Data received by the South African authorities that has been automatically exchanged under the CRS provides the first account of such data for an emerging economy. Periodically exchanged between January 2017 and March 2019, the available data contains account information transmitted from a total of 85 different exchanging jurisdictions, with the country coverage increasing over time. Apart from the jurisdiction where each account was incorporated, the data contains information on individual account balances, account types and the payment type and payment amounts into these accounts per transmission period. All amounts are expressed in the denominated currency of the respective account and converted into ZAR by SARS.

The use of CRS data for analytical purposes is not straight forward and requires a careful cleaning process. Upon inspection of the dataset, many duplicate entries emerge across anonymised tax identification numbers, detailed account balances and transmitting jurisdictions, which limit the usefulness of the data analysis and may distort estimations. The exact matching of CRS data to taxpayer records suggests a high probability of multiple transmission through the CRS of the same accounts. This fact is well-known to users of the data transferred under the CRS given the reporting requirements and has also been confirmed by authorities in other jurisdictions. To account for these data issues, entries are removed from the dataset wherever they are duplicated simultaneously by all three of the following: i) the anonymised tax identification number; ii) the account balance; and iii) the transmitting jurisdiction. Accounts by the same taxpayer in the same jurisdiction and with similar balances but denominated in different currencies are retained to take into account the fact that several accounts could have been opened with different financial institutions. Accounts with zero and very low holdings are also removed.[2] Payment flows, which sometimes are also transmitted multiple times for the same account, are separately cleaned for analysis to avoid double counting.[3]

Tables 6.1. and 6.2. provide basic summary statistics on the transmitted CRS accounts. During the period from January 2017 to March 2019, a total of six CRS transmissions took place between the South African authorities and exchanging jurisdictions, roughly falling into three consecutive tax years. The largest batches of accounts were exchanged always at the end of each year, respectively in December of 2017 and 2018. Smaller exchanges with relatively few accounts happened throughout this period. Overall coverage in terms of number of accounts, exchanging jurisdictions and total account balance shows an increasing trend, corresponding to enhanced commencement of AEOI by partner countries. A similar development is discernible for payments received for these accounts. Payments coverage, however, remains relatively patchy throughout the entire sample length.

Table 6.1. Summary statistics

Reporting period (aggregated per tax year)	Total individual account balances by exchanged accounts (in ZAR)	Total payments received by exchanged accounts (in ZAR)
2016/2017	43 935 723 088	4 378 935 011
2017/2018	758 753 600 174	72 309 396 394
2018/2019	1 061 920 373 073	138 109 424 924

Note: Total account balances and total payments aggregate all reported balances and payments into these accounts for the respective reporting period. Account balances and payments are expressed in ZAR.
Source: National Treasury.

Table 6.2. Total payments received by type

Reporting period (aggregated per tax year)	Interest (in ZAR)	Dividends (in ZAR)	Gross Proceeds / Redemptions (in ZAR)	Other (in ZAR)
2016/2017	25 037 689	925 476 406	1 418 339 247	2 010 081 668
2017/2018	2 221 279 909	1 850 131 570	59 109 022 944	9 128 961 970
2018/2019	2 417 951 360	2 761 639 171	120 142 664 863	12 787 170 530

Note: Payments by type into transferred accounts aggregated by reporting period. Payments are expressed in ZAR.
Source: National Treasury.

Due to the underlying data generation process determined by transmitting jurisdictions, data quality and information exchange requirements, the CRS data suffers from a few noteworthy limitations. Despite its broad geographic coverage, not all major jurisdictions participate in the CRS. This includes, for instance, the United States, which administers its own information exchange standard, FATCA. Moreover, account information is not always available, which may be due to poor quality documentation gathered by financial institutions or submitted to competent authorities. CRS data also reports only information on financial accounts; other forms of wealth storage such as real estate, art or crypto assets are currently outside its scope unless the proceeds of their sales have been deposited in a reported account. Information pertaining to these kind of investment activities outside the scope of CRS data could be cross-checked, for instance, with outflows data from the South African Reserve Bank (SARB).

The importance of IFC accounts in South Africa's CRS data

In December 2018, South Africans had over 585 000 accounts in 85 CRS-reporting jurisdictions abroad with a total account balance of about ZAR 1.26 trillion, an equivalent of about 20% of domestic GDP. The vast majority of these accounts, over 575 000, belonged to individuals (as opposed to entities). This means that individuals directly held about ZAR 1.06 trillion in financial assets offshore (Figure 6.1). IFCs accounted for less than half of all transmitting jurisdictions, but represent a majority of the balances of accounts exchanged. IFCs (37 jurisdictions total) reported about ZAR 897 billion (USD 67 billion) of South African assets from both individuals and corporates, corresponding to slightly more than 70% of all assets held by South Africans in foreign accounts exchanged under the CRS. When considering accounts owned by individuals only, the overall IFC balance reduces to about ZAR 748 billion (USD 56 billion), representing a similar share in all exchanged individual accounts. Total assets are highly concentrated among very few jurisdictions. In terms of total, individual and corporate account balances per jurisdiction, the top five IFC and non-IFC jurisdictions alone represent more than 80% of all assets in their respective group.

Figure 6.1. IFCs dominate account balances

Total account balances and account balances by individuals distributed by IFC and non-IFC jurisdictions

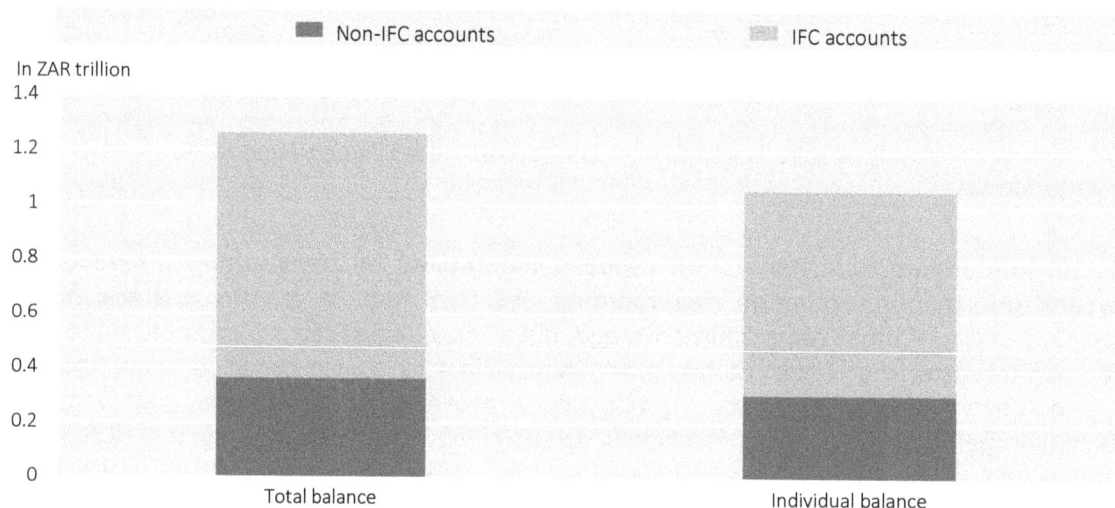

Note: The figure refers to the largest transmission of accounts on 31 December 2018. IFC jurisdictions refer to the list of IFCs established in O'Reilly, Parra Ramirez and Stemmer (2019[1]).
Source: National Treasury.

StatLink ▆▆ https://stat.link/vhxasb

Despite hosting the vast majority of South African assets abroad that are reported through the CRS, IFCs only account for 42% of all accounts exchanged. While, for instance, some OECD countries lead the list for hosting the most accounts in individual jurisdictions, several IFCs occupy top positions in terms of account balances exchanged alongside major trading partner jurisdictions. This discrepancy between a minority share in total number of accounts reported and a strong majority in total account balances exchanged means that very large average balances for individual and corporate accounts are held in several IFCs (Figure 6.2). While most of the accounts in non-IFC jurisdictions exhibit relatively high corporate and low individual balances, IFC accounts on average appear to be more balanced and report in a few cases larger individual deposits than corporate deposits.

Figure 6.2. IFCs dominate account balances of individuals and corporates

Average account balances of individuals and corporates per jurisdiction expressed in ZAR million

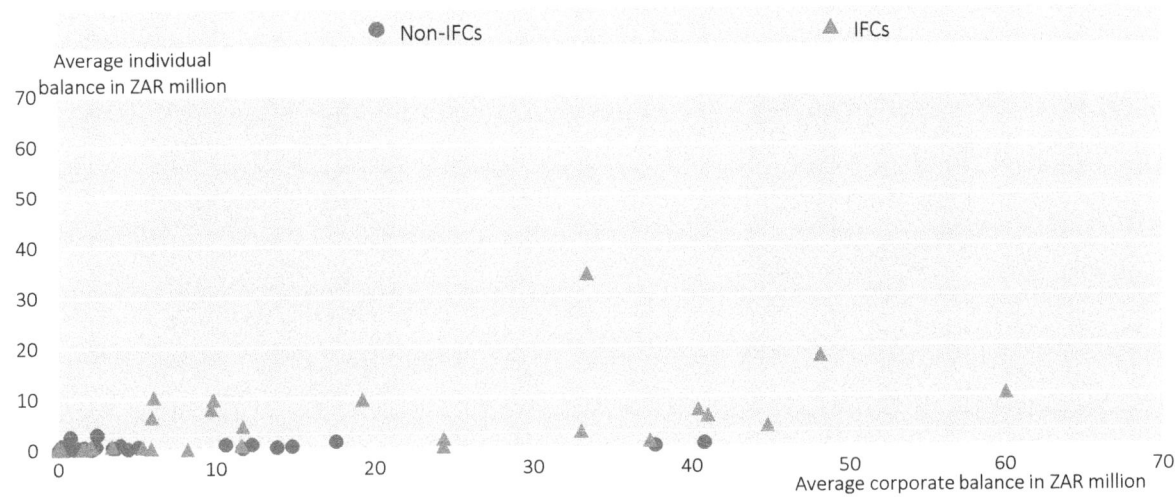

Note: Kuwait and Ireland are suppressed due to very high average corporate account balances.
Source: National Treasury.

StatLink ⟶ https://stat.link/zlpbyn

Average assets held by individuals and corporates in IFCs exhibit strong heterogeneity. Ranked by average account size for individuals, account balances range from more than USD 2.4 million (ZAR 35 million) at the upper end to below USD 100 (ZAR 1300), decreasing quickly among the top jurisdictions. Compared to total balances transmitted per jurisdiction, the order almost inverses, moving those with lower total balances but higher average balances to the top. A similar pattern emerges when only considering corporate accounts, with IFC jurisdictions confirming the more equal balance between individual and corporate account sizes. Interestingly, some of the top-ranked jurisdictions by account size have not played a major role as investment destinations in the SVDP, casting further doubt on the comprehensiveness of SVDP applications. Thus contrasting with expectations and theories on cross-border financial flow determinants (e.g. Fratzscher (2012[2])), the jurisdictions reporting the highest number of accounts and largest account balances do not necessarily coincide with country size, geographic proximity or economic integration with South Africa. Instead, they rather seem to point to capital flows to IFCs for tax non-compliance reasons (Casetta et al. (2014[3]), Haberly and Wójcik (2015[4])).

IFC jurisdictions seem to be the preferred destinations when for certain types of financial services. Apart from the almost equal share of unavailable account descriptions, IFCs predominantly transmitted accounts in relation to certain financial services such as, for instance, insurance contracts (Figure 6.3.). Non-IFCs in contrast provided the more mainstream banking services in form of deposits (IBAN/OBAN) or accounts and trusts for security investments (ISIN/OSIN), which together only make up about 10% of all accounts shared by IFCs. Account types in IFCs are thus different to declared offshore investments in the SVDP, where trusts and bank deposits dominate foreign accounts. These findings not only shed some light on IFC business practices but potentially suggest that the CRS data provides information on foreign accounts over and above what was disclosed by taxpayers in the existing VDP schemes.

Figure 6.3. Non-IFCs and IFCs differ in financial services provided

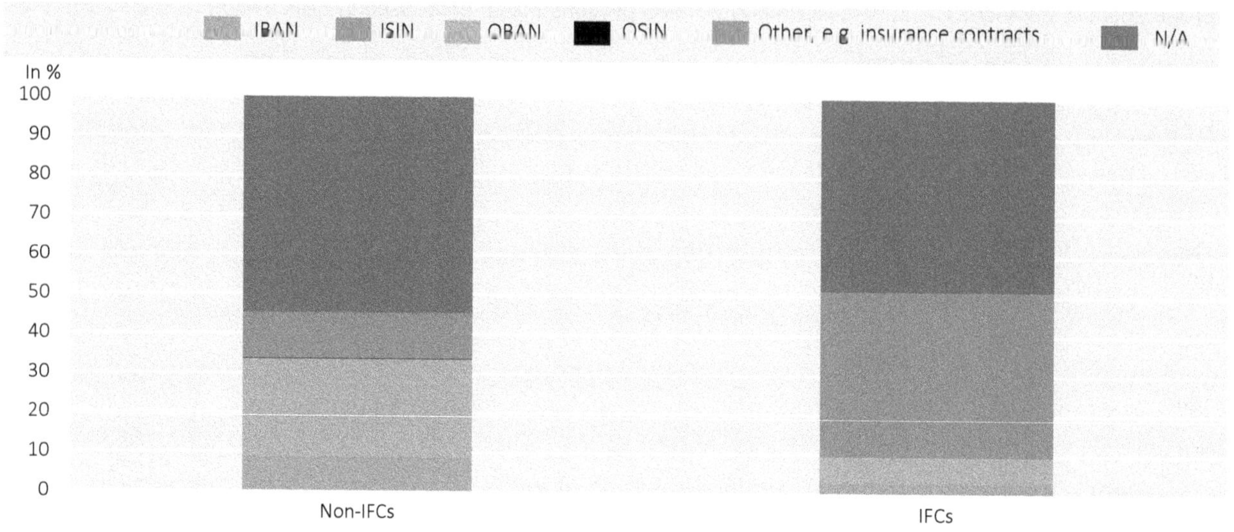

Note: The nomenclature of the CRS reporting messages refers to the different account descriptions respectively as IBAN (International Bank Account Number), ISIN (International Securities Information Number), OBAN (Other Bank Account Number), OSIN (Other Securities Information Number) and Other (any other type of account number. N/A refers to unavailable account descriptions.
Source: National Treasury.

StatLink https://stat.link/5nsm9e

Income tax compliance analysed through the CRS

Successfully linking CRS accounts with SARS income tax returns is an important step for ensuring taxpayer compliance and credibly increasing the risk that CRS information will lead to audits and penalties for non-complying taxpayers. Comparing the CRS data with income tax data from SARS shows that only about 43% of all accounts exchanged had a uniquely identifiable tax number for the 2018/2019 tax year. Perhaps surprisingly, IFC jurisdictions perform better in direct match rates compared to non-IFC jurisdictions. From those accounts with a tax number, around 86% can be directly matched with available income tax data from SARS. When only IFC jurisdictions are considered, around 56% of all accounts exhibit a corresponding tax number of which about 89% could be matched with SARS tax returns. As for non-IFC jurisdictions these percentage shares drop to around 35% for accounts with available tax numbers and 83% for direct matching rates. Assuming that all accounts exchanged under the CRS should theoretically correspond to taxpaying individuals, respectively only 37% of all foreign accounts and a bit less than half of all offshore accounts domiciled in IFCs could be easily assigned to South African taxpayers. There are a range of potential reasons why match rates may be low. They do not account for use of more advanced matching techniques such as fuzzy matching for example, which were not used as part of this project. Moreover, the CRS does not systematically require the reporting of tax numbers on foreign accounts whose existence preceded the introduction of the standard in the country, provided that reasonable efforts were undertaken to obtain them (OECD, 2021[5]).

Figure 6.4. Tax number availability and matching rates across jurisdictions

Percentage shares of individual accounts with tax numbers and matching rates with SARS income tax data

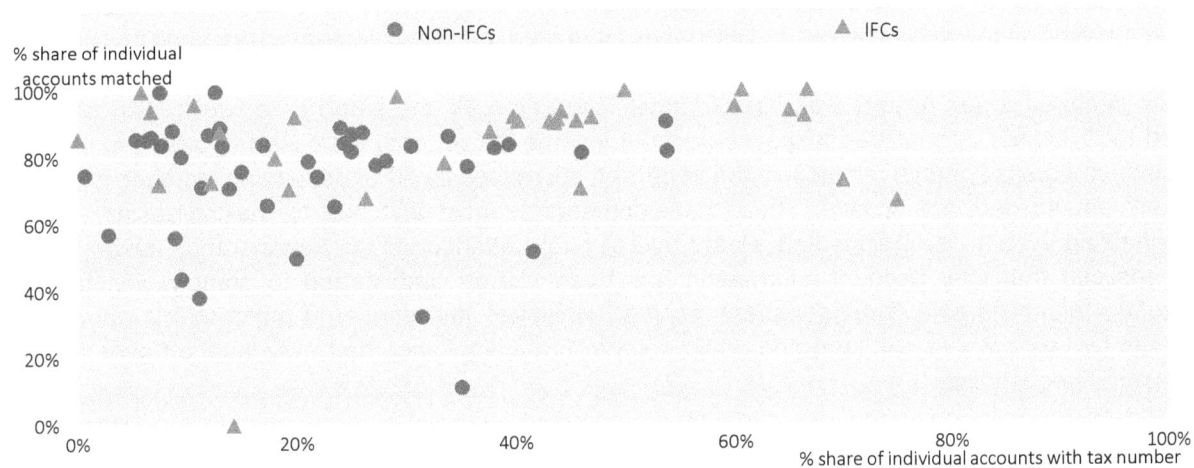

Source: National Treasury.

StatLink https://stat.link/4f6ep7

Despite these overall trends, jurisdictions display considerable heterogeneity in terms of individual tax number availability and matching rates with SARS data. Both diverge between IFCs and non-IFCs and vary between individual jurisdictions (Figure 6.4). Tax numbers are available for most IFC jurisdictions at relatively high percentage rates. Most IFCs also exhibit relatively high matching rates with SARS, for several jurisdictions match rates are at 100% of tax numbers available. In contrast, non-IFC jurisdictions exhibit in general a more heterogeneous picture. They range between less than 1% and slightly more than half of all accounts reporting assigned tax numbers, less than for some IFC jurisdictions. Resulting matching rates with tax returns are even more spread out and range from 13% with Estonia to 100% with Colombia, albeit for very few accounts.

VDP and SVDP applications can also be matched to CRS accounts. While all VDP applications achieved a matching rate with tax returns of close to 38%, the total of SVDP applications, successful or not, could be matched at a rate of slightly above 56%. The potential to achieve higher matching rates in collaboration with transferring jurisdictions and through use of more advanced matching techniques thus appears to be relatively large. Higher rates would thus not only increase transparency, but potentially also result in growing revenue collection. Although there is much room for improvement, the significantly higher matching rates between IFC accounts in CRS data and SARS tax returns are an encouraging sign for the efforts by tax authorities to trace foreign wealth back to its origin.

CRS account payments and income tax declarations

Matching tax returns with CRS accounts that received regular payments into these accounts complements the earlier analysis on taxpayer compliance. Of the 127 716 individuals with matching tax returns across all counterparty jurisdictions only 63 095 declared foreign capital income in the form of interest, dividends or capital gains. Considering income from dividends and interest declared, which would be taxable in South Africa after deducting any tax credits, the data suggest that around ZAR 530 million was identified through the CRS as being taxable in South Africa in the 2017/2018 tax year. In the subsequent tax year the amount of foreign interest and dividends identified in accounts exchanged with SARS rose sharply. Foreign dividends effectively declared increased from about ZAR 204 million to over ZAR 340 million and declared foreign interest rose from about ZAR 327 million to over ZAR 577 million.

A more detailed comparison between CRS payments and corresponding declared income taxes points to increasing compliance over time. There was a significant expansion in South Africa's AEOI network between 2018 and 2019, which shows in a significant rise in transmitted individual accounts and corresponding payment flows between the tax years 2018 and 2019. At the same time declared total incomes in relation to foreign interest and dividends increased relatively more than reported CRS payments (Figure 6.5). The difference between reported interest payments through the CRS and the amount of interest declared in tax returns was approximately the same. At the same time, while CRS payments related to dividends (of matched taxpayers without income tax returns) increased in proportion to rising account numbers, payments related to interest earned decreased by 50%, despite an increase in reported accounts (these data not shown). These developments suggest that due to the increasing reporting through rising CRS transmissions and related overall public attention to tax transparency, taxpayers may have realised that their account information has been shared and started to comply with tax laws, particularly with regards to foreign interest income.[4] However, the amount of matched but not declared accounts by taxpayers is still large and could point to non-compliance that may level off over time with increased detection risk.

Figure 6.5. Comparison of foreign capital income declarations with CRS account payments

Comparison by foreign capital income stream and tax year

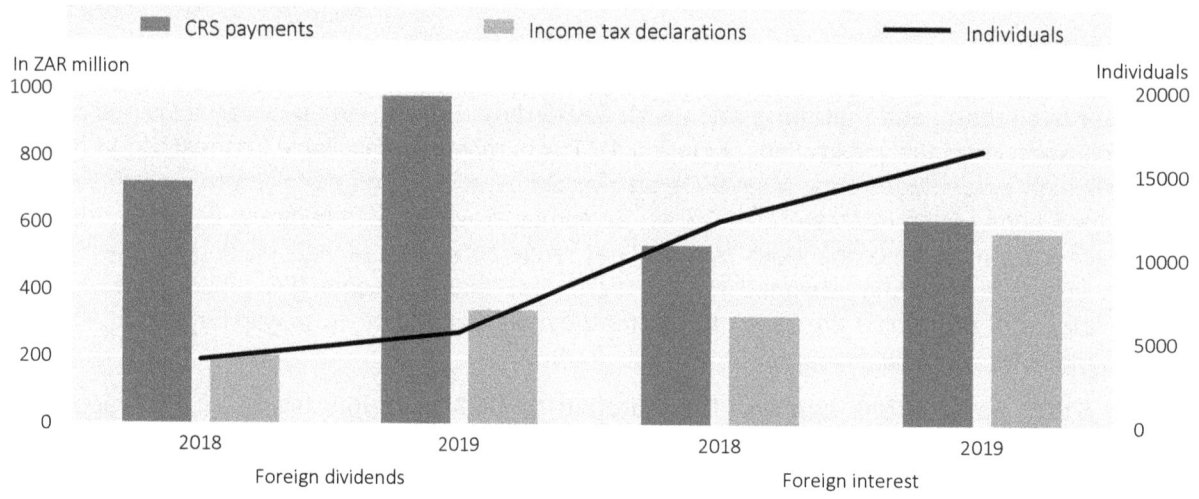

Source: National Treasury.

StatLink ⟶ https://stat.link/7zdvak

Findings in chapter 5 suggesting potentially ongoing non-compliance seem to be further corroborated by relating payment flows into CRS accounts with income tax declarations, ordered according to the taxpayer's position in the income distribution. Relative to their position in the income distribution, a substantial share of taxpayers in the middle-high income segment seemed to declare foreign capital income from interest and dividend payments (Figure 6.6). Increasing over the lower income distribution percentiles, most declarations were submitted between the 80% and the 99% percentile. However, declarations within the top 1% and particularly for the 0.1% decline substantially. This pattern mirrors offshore wealth declarations by taxable income in the SVDP (see Figure 5.15). If we are to assume that these patterns of reducing foreign income are not a result of different asset preferences by taxpayers at the very top of the income distribution, this may again suggest non- or under-declaration of foreign capital income by the very top income recipients.

Figure 6.6. Middle-high income individuals predominantly declared foreign capital income

CRS payment flows are merged with declared foreign capital income from interest and dividends

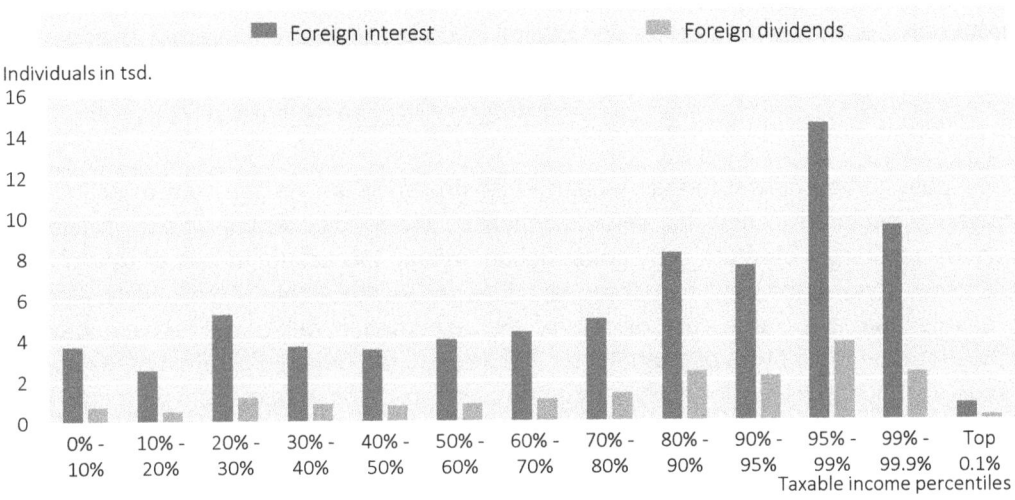

Note: Number of individuals that declared foreign capital income and appeared in the CRS data by taxable income percentiles.
Source: National Treasury.

StatLink ▨ https://stat.link/zdmeq2

Estimating past non-compliant offshore wealth and IFFs from tax data

The following section estimates previously non-compliant foreign wealth based on new income tax declarations and foreign account information transmitted under the CRS. Having adopted a definition of IFFs as cross-border financial flows that are illegal either in their origin, transfer or use, a key first step in understanding the amount of IFFs that have left South Africa illicitly involves estimating the amount of previously non-compliant foreign wealth. Owing to the different characteristics of the two data sources, estimations of non-compliant foreign wealth rely on two different methods: capitalising declared foreign income and estimating wealth from foreign financial account balances. After comparing the estimates from the two sources and evaluating their validity, the final step involves developing an estimate of the annual amount of IFFs derived from the non-compliant foreign wealth stock.

Capitalising declarations of foreign income

In general taxpayers' wealth can be estimated from income tax data. There is a large economic literature that seeks to carry out such estimations. To gauge the wealth distribution of US households indirectly, Greenwood (1983[6]), later Bricker et al. (2016[7]), Bricker et al. (2016b[8]) and Saez and Zucman (2016[9]), rely on a model that "capitalises" taxable income into wealth. Chatterjee et al. (2020[10]) and Orthofer (2016[11]) apply the same approach for estimating South Africa's wealth distribution. These models estimate financial wealth by inflating the different types of capital income from the underlying tax data by a general rate of return on assets associated with that income for a given year. Applied rates of return to the respective capital income category, for instance, can be estimated from annual market rates of return on different assets such as equity or Treasury bills. The resulting wealth estimates, however, are sensitive to taxable income definitions and model parameter selection. Careful consideration should thus be advised when interpreting any resulting estimates.

Given the availability of tax data on foreign income, this section approaches the estimation of undeclared South African foreign wealth by relying on the detailed and high quality data from the SARS-NT panel. The analysis gains in particular from the data on new tax report filings of foreign capital income peaking in 2017, as is shown in Figure 5.6 (Panel B). Past non-compliant foreign wealth is estimated from new tax declarations on foreign capital income derived from interest, dividends and capital gains as follows:

$$\widehat{Past\ non-compliant\ foreign\ wealth} = \sum_{\forall k} \frac{new\ declared\ foreign\ capital\ income_{k,t}}{r_{k,t}} \quad (1)$$

The estimated past non-compliant foreign wealth in South Africa is thus the sum of all individual foreign income streams k declared in new tax returns (interest, dividends, capital gains), capitalised by their respective asset-based rate of return r. By construction, raising the assumed rate of return would result in a respective lower amount of past non-compliant foreign wealth. While it is initially assumed that all underlying assets earn the same rate of return, the assumption could be relaxed later to allow for heterogeneous interest rates by investment type.[5][6] Moreover, the detailed position of taxpayers within the taxable income distribution allows for a more targeted analysis of those taxpayers who may be considered more likely to engage in evasion, i.e. the highest-income segments of the income distribution (Alstadsaeter, Johannesen and Zucman, 2018[12]).

Despite the quality of the data it must be recognised that any amounts of foreign assets inferred by capitalisation are heavily dependent on model parameters and estimates can be sensitive to small deviations in assumed rates of return. To alleviate these concerns, some precautions have been considered in the model. First, the results are estimated across a range of plausible rates of return taken from the literature. In their study of Norwegian taxpayer wealth, Fagareng et al. (2020[13]) estimate an average return to financial wealth of about 5% for the 90th percentile in the wealth distributions over the period 2005 - 2015. Jordà et al. (2019[14]) report a long-term average real rate of return to equities of 7% across a number of advanced economies. Thus in this analysis a rate of return of between 5% and 7% is assumed. These rates are assumed to be homogeneous for foreign interests, dividends and capital gains. Moreover, the analysis of declared foreign capital income by new tax report filings has shown a peak in declared amounts for new tax reports in 2017, coinciding with the South African commencement of active information exchange under the CRS. Thus new filings around that time may have particularly responded to the increasing risk of detection and can be assumed to be related to previously undeclared foreign wealth.

Based on the assumptions taken above, capitalising foreign capital income as declared in new tax returns yields between USD 0.4 billion and USD 0.9 billion in past undeclared foreign wealth. Figure 6.7 also separates out the year 2017 because it is particularly interesting for the analysis. More than two-thirds of that total amount estimated from new tax returns during 2012 – 2019 was provided by tax filers who declared for the first time in 2017, likely as a response to AEOI commencement. Independent of the rate of return assumed, the top 1% of income earners accounted for close to 70% of the total amount, of which the top 0.1% claimed about half. The accumulated wealth of lower percentiles only made up a fraction. While the estimated total amount needs to be validated by other data sources below and may suffer from non- or under-declarations of income, it nonetheless provides again evidence on the increased detection risk by EOI and the related responsiveness particularly by top income receivers.

Figure 6.7. Previously non-compliant offshore wealth imputed from returns by new tax filers

Analysis based on income capitalisation from tax declarations by new tax filers over time and per income percentile

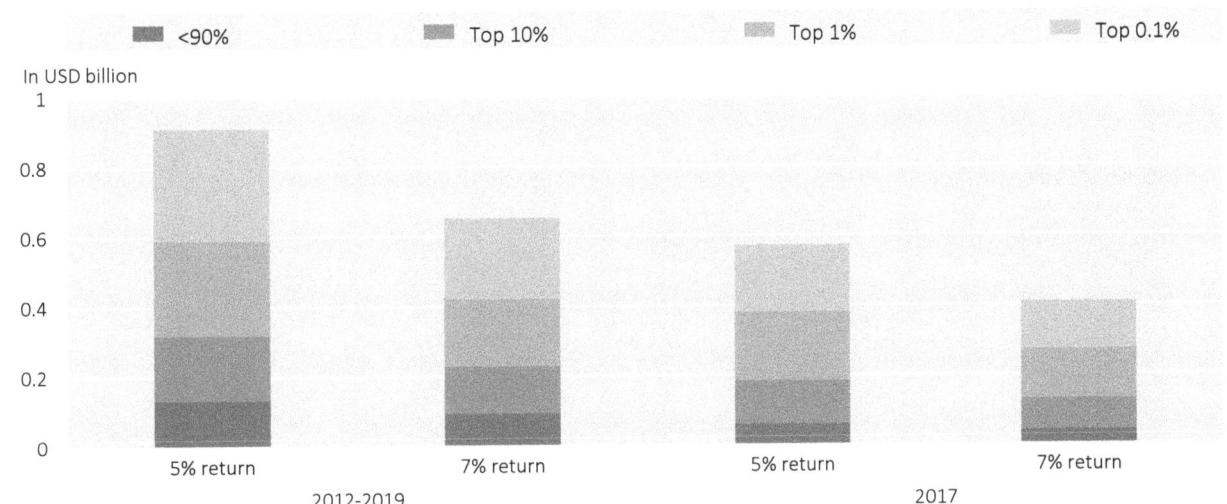

Note: The income tax declarations were converted from ZAR into USD using annual average exchange rates from the OECD database.
Source: Authors' calculations based on updated SARS-NT panel data (Ebrahim and Axelson, 2019[15]).

StatLink https://stat.link/gaudrp

Estimating past non-compliant offshore wealth and IFFs from CRS data

The comprehensive foreign account information exchanged under the CRS provides arguably the strongest source for estimating previously non-compliant offshore wealth in South Africa. This is not only due to the detailed data coverage but also the process of how the dataset has been established, which offer important advantages over other data sources. For instance, account balances transmitted from foreign jurisdictions offer third-party confirmation of taxpayers' financial wealth abroad. In contrast to self-declared taxpayer information such as, for instance, in income tax returns or the VDPs, data transmitted under the CRS has been reported to tax authorities and finance ministries by financial institutions. Therefore, despite potential inconsistencies or lack of diligence in reporting, especially in the early years of its implementation, the CRS data provides a very detailed picture of foreign assets owned by domestic taxpayers.

Despite the detailed coverage of foreign accounts, estimating previously non-compliant offshore wealth requires a number of important assumptions. The analysis is based on the key assumption that offshore wealth is predominantly located in IFC jurisdictions previously identified in O'Reilly, Parra Ramirez and Stemmer (2019[1]). Frequent reference to these jurisdictions in SVDP applications as preferred locations for undisclosed foreign assets lends further confidence to this assumption.

The appearance of IFC jurisdictions in SVDP applications and CRS data is similar. Across both datasets IFC jurisdictions show similar patterns in terms of individual jurisdictions appearing as well as their share of foreign accounts hosted relative to all reported SVDP and CRS accounts (Figure 6.8). The overall correlation of accounts reported in individual IFC jurisdictions stands at 0.6. For bank accounts alone, the most-referred-to investment category, the correlation is even higher, at 0.73. In contrast, most non-IFC jurisdictions only appear in CRS-exchanged data but do not tend to appear in the SVDP as shown by the blue dots on the x-axis. Non-IFC jurisdictions may have also facilitated taxpayer non-compliance at some point in the past. However, these jurisdictions have been more deeply embedded in multilateral regulatory frameworks and transparency initiatives that render such behaviour relatively less likely on an ongoing basis.

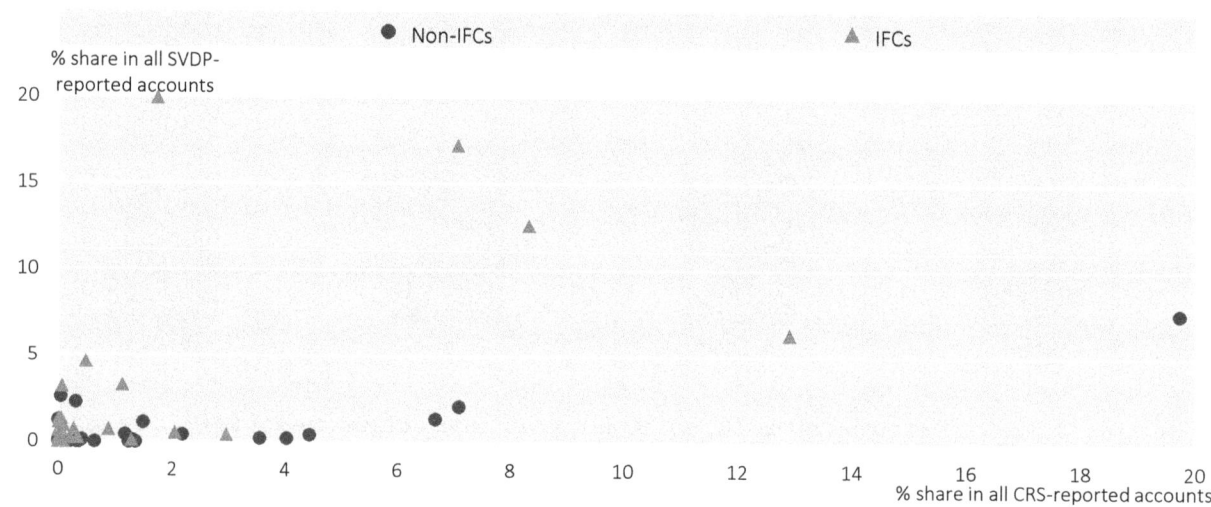

Figure 6.8. The high frequency of IFC jurisdictions in SVDP and CRS data

Shares of hosted accounts in IFC and non-IFC jurisdictions relative to all hosted foreign accounts

Note: Shares are calculated against total accounts reported in the SVDP or CRS.
Source: National Treasury.

StatLink https://stat.link/83vwok

Moreover, even though previous hidden offshore wealth is expected to be held in IFCs, assets invested in these jurisdictions may not necessarily have been non-compliant with tax laws. Assumptions on non-compliant shares of offshore wealth are thus based on existing evidence from the literature and compared to CRS matching rates with income tax returns and VDP/SVDP applications. Evidence from several countries on cross-border financial accounts reports estimates on non-compliance of assets invested in IFCs ranging from as low as 60% - 80% (Pellegrini, Sanelli and Tosti, 2016[16]) up to 85% - 95% (Alstadsaeter, Johannesen and Zucman (2019[17]); United States Senate (2014[18])).

Matching rates between CRS accounts and income tax returns by tax identification number do not necessarily provide direct evidence of past compliance of existing accounts. For instance, the transmission of tax identification numbers for accounts that existed prior to CRS implementation in the respective countries is not always required. However, successfully matched accounts may provide information on taxpayers that were already available to tax authorities at some point in the past, including accounts that may have already been declared. As described above, all CRS accounts received by South Africa exhibit an effective matching rate of around 37%, thus potentially up to 63% may have been unknown to SARS. The corresponding rate for IFC accounts is about 50%. Beyond successful matching, these rates may also include other information available to SARS on foreign accounts prior to information exchange. Against this background, an alleged non-compliance share of 85% - 95% on all foreign wealth suggested by some of the academic literature appears to be too high. As a result, all foreign wealth estimates are expressed under the assumption of past non-compliance rates of within bounds of 60% to 80% (the lower end of the estimates provided in the academic literature).

Despite the diligence in taking reasonable assumptions, the estimations are subject to a number of caveats that need to be considered. First, the transmitted account data is subject to a data cleaning process as described above, which could create the risk of mistakenly discarding observations. According to the applied process, simultaneous duplicates across the different account characteristics such as taxpayer identification numbers, reporting jurisdictions, account balances but also denominated currency and payment flows have been removed. Second, CRS reporting from financial institutions may not be comprehensive due to, for instance, technical capacity issues or limited data available to the institution on account holders, which may particularly occur with older accounts. This would result in an already incomplete dataset transferred to the South African authorities. Third, CRS avoidance cannot be taken into account and IFFs may have also left to non-IFC jurisdictions. However, the observed frequent reference to IFC jurisdictions both in the SVDP applications and CRS data makes their selection as potential destinations to hide non-compliant assets at least highly plausible. Fourth, wealth shifted out of South Africa due to IFFs may have been spent by taxpayers. Finally, wealth may be held overseas in forms of wealth not currently covered by information exchange agreements, such as art, real estate, or cryptoassets.

Estimating heretofore undeclared offshore wealth follows the process below, which is also schematically presented in Figure 6.9:

1. In a first step, reported total and individual account balances are assessed and cleaned. Simultaneous duplicated entries by anonymised identification number, account balances and transmitting jurisdictions are suppressed.[7] Accounts by the same taxpayer in the same jurisdictions but denominated in different currencies are retained. Total account balances with positive asset holdings are aggregated per jurisdiction and converted from ZAR into USD.

2. The second step involves the aggregation of total and individual account balances from IFC jurisdictions only. Out of the 47 IFC jurisdictions identified in O'Reilly, Parra Ramirez and Stemmer (2019[1]), 37 report active accounts to South African authorities.

3. Third, the aggregated account balances from IFCs are multiplied by estimates of non-disclosure probability for offshore accounts of between 60% - 80% in accordance with evidence from the literature and SARS data.

Figure 6.9. Estimating hitherto undeclared offshore wealth from CRS accounts

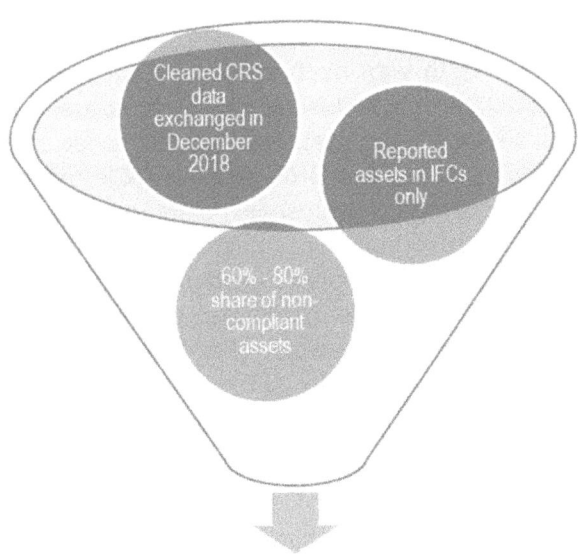

Total account balances: USD 40.4 billion - USD 53.8 billion
Total account balances by individuals: USD 33.7 billion – USD 44.9 billion

Note: Account balances in ZAR have been converted into USD according to the average ZAR-USD exchange rate in 2018 (OECD, 2021).
Source: National Treasury.

According to exchanged CRS accounts in December 2018, historically non-compliant total assets invested offshore range between USD 40.4 billion and USD 53.8 billion, an equivalent of about 10% to 15% of South African GDP. Total assets held abroad only by individuals amount to between USD 33.7 billion and USD 44.9 billion.

Compared to estimations relying on new tax declarations, past non-compliant offshore wealth estimates through the CRS are about forty to fifty times larger. Previously undeclared foreign wealth based on capitalising foreign capital income from new tax declarations in the SARS-NT panel only ranges between about USD 0.4 billion and USD 0.9 billion. The differences in estimated size hail largely from the unprecedented detailed coverage of foreign account data in the CRS in terms of financial account balances and geographic reach, particularly of IFCs. The CRS data has been third-party validated and does not rely on self-declarations of foreign capital income or assets invested abroad. Discrepancies may further arise due to substantial non-declaration or underreporting of foreign income by taxpayers when largely relying on self-declared income tax data. This suggests that the CRS data may provide substantial additional data to tax authorities relative to existing data. Underlying technical differences in cleaning and assembling the income tax datasets based on varying matching parameters may also add challenges to the estimation process.

Given that the above estimate relies on unprecedented data from the CRS, the reported amounts need to be set into perspective relative to global estimates reported elsewhere in the literature. For instance, Alstadsaeter et al. (2018[12]) estimate, based on data from 2007, that around 11.8% of South African GDP is invested in undeclared assets in IFCs abroad. By relying also on tax data, more recent evidence from Colombia shows that around 15% of GDP as an upper bound was held in non-compliant offshore wealth (Londoño-Vélez and Ávila-Mahecha, 2021[19]). Both shares reported in the literature are remarkably similar to what has been found for South Africa based on CRS data. These findings imply that while the degree of tax non-compliance appears to have grown in the past relative to economic activity, South Africa's experience with tax evasion and IFFs seems to be of a similar order or magnitude to other jurisdictions.

From non-compliant wealth stocks to illicit financial flows

Previously undeclared offshore wealth was likely the result of past financial outflows.[8] The final step to use tax data to quantify annual IFFs thus requires linking the estimated stocks of previously undeclared offshore wealth to these flows in the past. The approach used in this analysis is different to the rest of the literature, largely owing to the unique CRS data available on the stock of financial assets in foreign accounts. While the rest of the literature assesses the aggregate flows directly, largely trade flows, and asks 'what fractions are illicit', this report examines offshore wealth stocks, estimates a fraction that is illicit and asks 'what flows could generate this share'. This has the advantage of being agnostic as to the nature of the flows. The assumption here is that, regardless of the specific illicit method through which flows left South Africa (e.g. smuggling, trade mis-invoicing, or fraudulent payments, etc.), all the flows that left result in wealth that is not declared to tax authorities.[9]

Backing out annual IFFs from past non-compliant offshore wealth requires some final assumptions regarding the duration of yearly outflows and the rate of annual return to these flows abroad. As before, evidence from the literature and the present data analysis is used to generate these estimates. As to the nature of the underlying annual rate of return, this exercise relies as a baseline on evidence provided by Fagareng et al. (2020[13]) who report average real returns of about 5% to foreign assets that is used elsewhere in this chapter. Slightly higher real rates of return on equity of about 7% are reported by Jordà et al. (2019[14]). A change in the underlying return has, as will be shown below, only a marginal effect on the estimate of annual IFFs. Regarding the assumed duration of annual outflows, applications to the VDP/SVDP and periods of non-compliance declared therein provide a reasonable benchmark. Continued annual outflows over a period of 10 years (the average length of non-compliance provided in the SVDP data) is therefore the hypothesis used.

These assumptions applied to the previously estimated undeclared offshore wealth in the past result in IFFs in South Africa of between around USD 3.5 billion and USD 5 billion per year. The red-shaded areas in Figure 6.10 show the range of estimated annual IFFs taking into consideration the discussed share of 60% – 80% non-compliance in past undeclared offshore wealth and the 10-year period of consecutive outflows. To provide some initial robustness, different real rates of return to flows invested abroad have been applied. Panel A presents results for a 5% annual return to assets, Panel B for a 7% return to assets. The different horizontal lines outside the shaded area represent respectively lower (50%) or higher assumptions (95%) on non-compliance which can be considered less likely given available data. As Figure 6.10 also shows, increasing the assumed real rate of return from 5% to 7% alters the IFF trajectories only slightly by marginally decreasing estimated IFFs at the lower bound.

Figure 6.10. Estimates of annual IFF outflows

Estimated annual IFF outflows conditional on the level of non-compliance and rate of return to investments

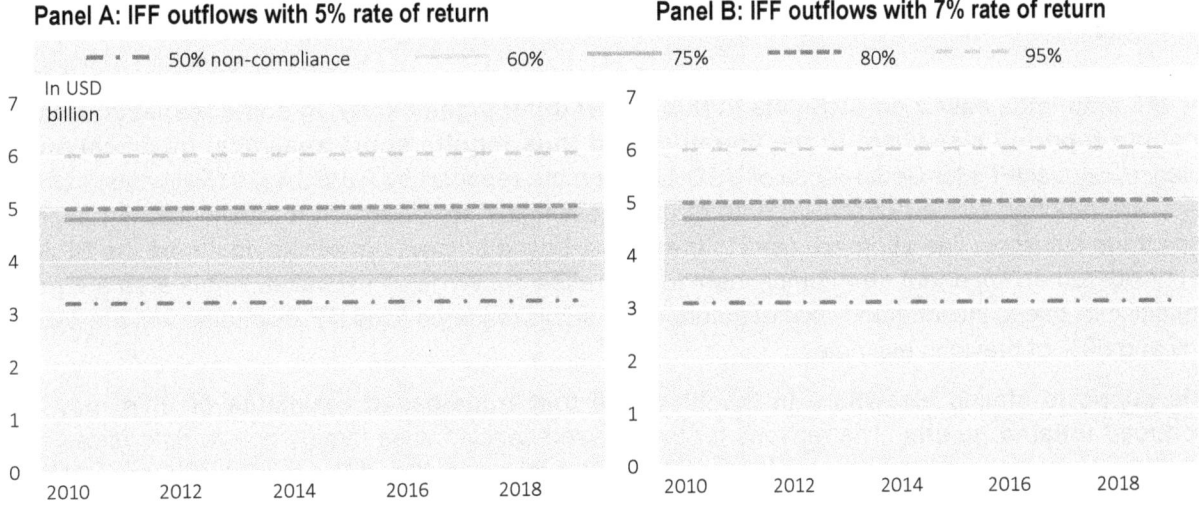

Note: The red-shaded area shows the likely range of estimated annual IFFs taking into consideration plausible shares of non-compliance in previously undeclared offshore wealth, real rates of return to flows invested abroad and the time period of consecutive outflows. The different lines represent lower or higher assumptions on non-compliance which are not confirmed by available data.
Source: National Treasury.

StatLink https://stat.link/kbag8x

Figure 6.11 shows a more thorough sensitivity analysis of the IFF estimates. While the estimated amount of non-compliant wealth held offshore remains fixed, the heat map below provides more detailed projections of past annual outflows for different years of duration, rates of return and assumed degrees of non-compliance. Coloured from light green to dark red and increasing in size, the fields represent likelihoods of IFF outflows in line with and exceeding the identified data-driven assumptions. The green fields in the middle panel show the headline results presented above for annual IFFs ranging between USD 3.5 billion and USD 5 billion, assuming a 10-year duration of outflows, a 60% - 80% degree of non-compliance and 5% or 7% rates of return. All other green-coloured fields fall within this range of annual flows, even when considering, for instance, very high rates of return of 10% and continuous financial outflows for up to 15 years. The red-shaded areas can be considered to be less likely given the adopted parameter mix. The observed stability of the estimates for the identified IFF range of annual outflows across a wide range of parameters lends some confidence in the adopted estimation strategy and obtained results.

Figure 6.11. Sensitivity analysis to IFF estimates

Estimated annual IFF outflows across different lengths of outflow duration, rates of return and non-compliance

Duration	8 years			10 years			15 years		
Rate of return / Non-compliance	5%	7%	10%	5%	7%	10%	5%	7%	10%
50%	4	3.9	3.8	3.2	3.1	3	2.1	2.1	2
60%	4.7	4.6	4.5	3.8	3.7	3.6	2.5	2.5	2.4
75%	5.8	5.8	5.6	4.8	4.7	4.6	3.2	3.1	3
80%	6.3	6.3	6	5	5	4.9	3.4	3.3	3.2
95%	7.5	7.5	7.2	6.1	6	5.8	4.1	4	3.9

Note: The robustness of IFF estimates is checked across different lengths of outflow duration, rates of return and degree of non-compliance in relation to foreign assets. The green-shaded cells fall within the previously identified range of annual outflows and can thus be considered as more likely in size than the red-shaded, higher estimates.
Source: National Treasury.

StatLink https://stat.link/a1fwke

The IFF estimates based on CRS data in this report differ significantly, in some respects, from the amounts reported elsewhere in the literature and thus require some analytical qualification. For instance, annual IFFs for South Africa of USD 14 billion are reported by AU/ECA (2015[20]) and of USD 20 billion are reported by GFI (2021[21]). Both of these estimates are based on a totally different approach using trade statistics. The approach used in this report, based on newly-available data from the CRS, can be considered an important new complement to this research. While all estimates in this area are fraught with difficulty due to the inherently secret nature of IFFs, this research finds IFF estimates that are between 17% and 50% of previous estimates.

This supports claims elsewhere in the literature that trade-based estimates of IFFs may have produced inflated results. The reasons for these discrepancies arise largely due to differences in the data used, arbitrary assumptions, and estimation approaches applied. Most recent studies ((AU/ECA, 2015[20]), (Global Financial Integrity, 2021[21]), (UNCTAD, 2020[22]), (Signé, Sow and Madden, 2020[23])) are based on aggregated trade data to estimate a total amount of IFFs having left the country or the entire Sub-Saharan region on an annual basis. These estimations, attempting to calculate trade mis-invoicing, rely on trade gap analysis by exploiting data mismatches in partner-country trade statistics. Sometimes residuals from balance of payments statistics are added as an additional factor to account for remaining potential outflows. Relying on such aggregated data may likely inflate results and leaves little analytical space for disentangling IFFs into their subcomponents, which is important in a country-specific context.

In contrast, the present analysis uses tax data to provide a new estimate of IFFs. For this report these IFFs constitute cross-border financial flows that have not been declared to tax authorities and are illegal either in their origin, transfer or use. Despite relying on data-driven assumptions, the analysis does not rely on data gaps in international statistics but on an important extension of them: a novel and unique form of tax microdata reporting foreign financial accounts. As a result of the defined focus of this report, other IFF components within the tax and commercial space such as smuggling or money laundering have not been separately assessed in detail. However, the CRS relates to all the different illicit outflows to a certain extent. Whenever IFFs or subsequent non-compliant investments from financial flows end up in foreign financial accounts and are invested in reportable assets by tax residents in the country of their origin, they will become subject to information exchange and could be detected.

Results and policy implications

This chapter has estimated annual IFFs based on the assessment of previously non-compliant offshore wealth. Detailed financial account data exchanged under the CRS between South Africa and foreign jurisdictions has provided the background for a careful analysis of previously non-compliant financial assets held abroad as well as preceding IFF outflows. Due to the comprehensive and detailed coverage of foreign financial accounts, estimations with CRS data have allowed for a broader picture to be provided of previously non-compliant foreign wealth. Based on data cleaning and well-founded assumptions based on the economic literature and other data used in this study regarding potential non-compliance and returns to foreign assets, it is estimated that past total undeclared foreign wealth of South Africans invested in IFCs amounts to between USD 40.4 billion and USD 53.8 billion. Over a period of ten years, this amount would result in preceding illicit financial outflows of approximately between USD 3.5 to USD 5 billion annually. While these flows are still substantial, the analysis suggests that some existing estimates of annual IFFs for South Africa may have produced inflated results and exceed the estimated yearly flows in this report by four to five times the amount.

The CRS enhances the scope of data analysis on tax non-compliance and brings increasing transparency to global hidden wealth. It also provides new insights into overall cross-border financial activity of a country's taxpayers. In December 2018, South Africans held over 585 000 accounts in 85 jurisdictions abroad with a total account balance of about ZAR 1.26 trillion. This implies that the total amount of account balances held outside the country by taxpayers represents more than 20% of the country's GDP. Less than half of these accounts were domiciled in IFCs but accounted for about 70% of all exchanged account balances.

Successfully linking CRS accounts with SARS income returns is a key step in credibly increasing both the risk for disclosure and revenue collection potential. Linking the CRS data with income tax data from SARS reveals that only about 30% of all accounts exchanged under the CRS had a uniquely identifiable tax number in tax year 2019. From those accounts with a tax number around 87% could be matched with available income tax data from SARS, resulting in effective matching of a little more than 35% of all accounts. In contrast, the effective matching rate with income tax returns for IFC accounts is slightly less than half of all transmitted accounts. These rates leave room for significant improvement with regard to effective assessment, which has the potential to result in revenue collection gains in the future.

A more detailed comparison between CRS payments and declared income taxes suggests increasing compliance over time. Between 2018 and 2019, declared total incomes in relation to foreign interest and dividends increased relatively more than reported CRS payments for interest and dividends. These developments suggest that amid rising account transmissions over time taxpayers may have realised that their account information has been shared and improved their tax compliance, particularly with regards to foreign interest income. Moreover, relative to their position in the income distribution, a substantial share of taxpayers in the middle-high income segment declared foreign capital income from interest and dividend payments. However, the number of matched but not declaring taxpayers is still large and points to non-compliance that may level off over time due to increased detection risk, presumably also driven by more declarations from high-income earners.

The analysis has proven that exchanged CRS information can provide new insights above and beyond other available data sources in terms of individual cross-border finance and can become an essential tool in the fight against tax evasion and IFFs. Its effective use, however, depends on the tax administration capacity to exploit the information transmitted. On the analytical side, this requires a strengthening of data processing capacity across agencies that allows them to increasingly link foreign account data with available tax returns. Moreover, the regulatory framework needs to be constantly revised and updated to enable a smooth transmission of foreign account information amid an enlarging multilateral AEOI network.

References

Alstadsaeter, A., N. Johannesen and G. Zucman (2019), "Tax Evasion and Inequality", *American Economic Review*, Vol. 109/6, pp. 2073-2103. [17]

Alstadsaeter, A., N. Johannesen and G. Zucman (2018), "Who owns the wealth in tax havens? Macro evidence and implications for global inequality", *Journal of Public Economics*, Vol. 162, pp. 89-100, https://doi.org/10.1016/j.jpubeco.2018.01.008. [12]

AU/ECA (2015), *Track it! Stop it! Get it! Report of the High Level Panel of Illicit Financial Flows from Africa*, https://repository.uneca.org/bitstream/handle/10855/22695/b11524868.pdf?sequence=3&isAllowed=y. [20]

Bricker, J. et al. (2016), "Estimating Top Income and Wealth Shares: Sensitivity to Data and Methods", *American Economic Review: Papers & Proceedings*, Vol. 106/5, pp. 641-645, http://dx.doi.org/10.1257/aer.p20161020. [7]

Bricker, J. et al. (2016b), "Measuring Income and Wealth at the Top Using Administrative and Survey Data", *Brookings Papers on Economic Activity*, Vol. Spring, pp. 261-331, https://www.brookings.edu/wp-content/uploads/2016/03/brickertextspring16bpea.pdf. [8]

Casetta, A. et al. (2014), "Financial flows to tax havens: Determinants and anomalies", *Quaderni dell'antiriciclaggio*, Vol. 1/March 2014, https://uif.bancaditalia.it/pubblicazioni/quaderni/2014/quaderni-analisi-studi-2014-1/Quaderno_Analisi_studi_1.pdf?language_id=1. [3]

Chatterjee, A., L. Czajka and A. Gethin (2020), "Estimating the distribution of household wealth in South Africa", *UNU-WIDER Working Paper 45*, https://doi.org/10.35188/UNU-WIDER/2020/802-3. [10]

Ebrahim, A. and C. Axelson (2019), "The creation of an individual level panel using administrative tax microdata in South Africa", *UNU-WIDER Working Paper 661-6*, https://doi.org/10.35188/UNU-WIDER/2019/661-6. [15]

Fagareng, A. et al. (2020), "Heterogeneity and Persistence in Returns to Wealth", *Econometrica*, Vol. 88/1, pp. 115-170, https://doi.org/10.3982/ECTA14835. [13]

Fratzscher, M. (2012), "Capital flows, push versus pull factors and the global financial crisis", *Journal of International Economics*, Vol. 88/2, pp. 341-356, https://doi.org/10.1016/j.jinteco.2012.05.003. [2]

Global Financial Integrity (2021), *Trade-Related Illicit Financial Flows in 134 Developing Countries: 2009-2018*, https://secureservercdn.net/50.62.198.97/34n.8bd.myftpupload.com/wp-content/uploads/2021/12/IFFs-Report-2021.pdf?time=1643653304. [21]

Greenwood, D. (1983), "An Estimation of U.S. Family Welath and Its Distribution From Microdata, 1973", *The Review of Income and Wealth*, Vol. 29/1, pp. 23-44, https://doi.org/10.1111/j.1475-4991.1983.tb00630.x. [6]

Haberly, D. and D. Wójcik (2015), "Tax havens and the production of offshore FDI: an empirical analysis", *Journal of Economic Geography*, Vol. 15, pp. 75-101, https://doi.org/10.1093/jeg/lbu003. [4]

Jordà, Ò. et al. (2019), "The Rate of Return on Everything, 1870–2015", *The Quarterly Journal of Economics*, Vol. 134/3, pp. 1225–1298, https://doi.org/10.1093/qje/qjz012. [14]

Leenders, W. et al. (2020), "Offshore Tax Evasion and Wealth Inequality: Evidence from a Tax Amnesty in the Netherlands", *EconPol Working Paper 52*, Vol. 4, https://www.ifo.de/DocDL/EconPol_Working_Paper_52_Offshore_Tax_Evasion.pdf. [25]

Londoño-Vélez, J. and J. Ávila-Mahecha (2021), "Enforcing Wealth Taxes in the Developing World: Quasi-Experimental Evidence from Colombia", *American Economic Review: Insights*, Vol. 3/2, pp. 131-148, https://doi.org/10.1257/aeri.20200319. [19]

O'Reilly, P., K. Parra Ramirez and M. Stemmer (2019), "Exchange of information and bank deposits in international financial centres", *OECD Taxation Working Papers*, No. 46, OECD Publishing, Paris, https://dx.doi.org/10.1787/025bfebe-en. [1]

OECD (2021), *Global Forum on Transparency and Exchange of Information for Tax Purposes: Toolkit for the Implementation of the Standard for Automatic Exchange of Financial Account Information*, OECD Publishing, https://www.oecd.org/tax/transparency/documents/aeoi-implementation-toolkit_en.pdf. [5]

Orthofer, A. (2016), "Wealth inequality in South Africa: Evidence from survey and tax data", *REDI3x3 Working Paper 15*, http://redi3x3.org/sites/default/files/Orthofer%202016%20REDI3x3%20Working%20Paper%2015%20-%20Wealth%20inequality.pdf. [11]

Pellegrini, V., A. Sanelli and E. Tosti (2016), "What do External Statistics tell us About Undeclared Assets held Abroad and Tax Evasion?", *Bank of Italy Occasional Paper No. 367*, https://papers.ssrn.com/sol3/papers.cfm?abstract_id=2917184. [16]

Saez, E. and G. Zucman (2016), "Wealth Inequality in the United States since 1913: Evidence from Capitalized Income Tax Data", *The Quarterly Journal of Economics*, Vol. 131/2, pp. 519-578, https://doi.org/10.1093/qje/qjw004. [9]

Signé, L., M. Sow and P. Madden (2020), *Illicit financial flows in Africa: Drivers, destinations, and policy options*, https://www.brookings.edu/wp-content/uploads/2020/02/Illicit-financial-flows-in-Africa.pdf. [23]

UNCTAD (2020), *Tackling Illicit Financial Flows for Sustainable Development in Africa*, United Nations Publications, https://unctad.org/system/files/official-document/aldcafrica2020_en.pdf. [22]

United States Senate (2014), *Offshore Tax Evasion: The Effort to Collect Unpaid Taxes on Billions in Hidden Offshore Accounts*, https://www.hsgac.senate.gov/imo/media/doc/REPORT%20-%20OFFSHORE%20TAX%20EVASION%20(Feb%2026%202014,%208-20-14%20FINAL).pdf. [18]

Zucman, G. (2013), "THE MISSING WEALTH OF NATIONS: ARE EUROPE AND THE U.S. NET DEBTORSS OR NET CREDITORS?", *The Quarterly Journal of Economic*, pp. 1321–1364, https://doi.org/10.1093/qje/qjt012. [24]

Notes

[1] OECD staff thanks the National Treasury, particularly Chris Axelson, for his analysis of South Africa's CRS data.

[2] There is a relatively small probability that not all transferred accounts belong to South African tax residents. For instance, some accounts may be dormant, as a change in residency by the account holder may have not been reported to the managing financial institution. Zero and low-balance accounts have thus been dropped to account for this potential issue in the transmitted data.

[3] While observations that contain duplicated combinations of anonymised taxpayer identification numbers (TIN), reporting jurisdictions, and account balances are removed, double entries accounting for reported payments have also been assessed in a second step. All else equal, this would remove some payment line items into the same accounts but would not affect the total account balance used for the IFF estimation.

[4] These trends are also reflected when attempting to calculate the tax loss by adding the non-declared amount to taxable income. Since it can only be estimated for linked records where income is declared as interest or dividends, the tax loss appears to be at a minimum around ZAR 770 million in 2018 and ZAR 540 million in 2019. These amounts, however, exclude the large categories for income of "Other" and "Gross proceeds/Redemptions".

[5] In contrast to Bricker et al. (2016b[8]) or Greenwood (1983[6]) the analysis does not aim to estimate total wealth but rather concentrates on the amount of foreign accumulated assets corresponding to the respective foreign income flows as declared in new tax returns. A variable that accounts for estimated non-financial wealth such as, for instance, housing wealth, is therefore not added.

[6] A similar approach to gauge hidden wealth has been employed by Leenders et al. (2020[25]) who rely on taxes collected from disclosed offshore wealth. However, given the imprecise allocation of taxes and levies collected to the respective self-declared offshore assets, this report relies on the income capitalisation method following Bricker et al. (2016b[8]).

[7] While duplicates of anonymised taxpayer identification number (TIN), reporting jurisdiction and account balance combinations are suppressed, double entries accounting for reported payments have also been assessed in a second step. All else equal, this would remove some payment line items into the same accounts but do not affect the total account balance used for the IFF estimation.

[8] While the accounts abroad could have also been filled with capital inflows from elsewhere, these accounts have nonetheless been transferred to SARS as registered abroad by South African taxpayers. It can thus be considered as very likely that the initial flows generating these offshore assets also had their origin in South Africa.

[9] Although related, the approach in this report takes the opposite direction of the wealth accounting framework used for instance in Zucman (2013[24]). There, past investment flows are cumulated to estimate wealth while valuation effects are accounted for. Here, new data on wealth is used to estimate past flows.

7 Summary and key recommendations

This report presents results from a joint project between the OECD and South Africa National Treasury, which assesses tax compliance and IFFs in South Africa. The present analysis evaluates the impact of recent tax compliance initiatives, where continuing gaps remain, and provides estimates of historical non-compliant foreign wealth and resulting illicit outflows. Based on a variety of unique anonymised individual tax data, most importantly foreign financial accounts exchanged under the CRS, the project not only provides an order of magnitude of IFFs from South Africa in recent years but also evaluates the behaviour of taxpayers facing increasing global and domestic tax transparency.

The analysis comes at a crucial juncture for South Africa. The country faces significant fiscal and socio-economic challenges, which have been exacerbated by the ongoing COVID-19 pandemic. While extensive fiscal measures have helped to mitigate the pandemic fallout, they have contributed to the build-up of contingent liabilities and may put debt sustainability at further risk. At the same time spending pressures are mounting to fund short-term policies but also achieve more resilience in the long term as envisioned by the SDGs. Successfully curtailing IFFs, combatting tax evasion, and expanding the tax base are therefore important elements to foster domestic resource mobilisation and to increase the potential for revenue growth.

The analysis reveals that tax evasion has a long history in South Africa and has been concentrated among the very wealthy and top income recipients. In 2018, estimated non-compliant assets worth between USD 40 billion and USD 54 billion were held in IFCs relying on cross-border financial account data from the CRS. Based on these figures, the analysis estimates that these deposits could be associated with annual IFFs of between USD 3.5 billion and USD 5 billion per year over the last decade. While this analysis is also subject to well-founded assumptions, it is based on new data of foreign financial assets that has never before been used in the assessment of IFFs, which allows for a more granular assessment of IFFs as well as a tailored methodology. Combatting IFFs in South Africa will thus significantly contribute to increasing tax revenues and financing the country's continued economic development, but this analysis suggests that this will likely be to a lesser extent than suggested by some other estimates of IFFs, reported by, for instance, AU/ECA (2015[1]) and GFI (2021[2]).

The analysis shows that important progress has been made in enhancing taxpayer compliance in recent years. Examining taxpayer data, revenue source data and data from voluntary disclosure programmes shows evidence of increasing taxpayer compliance and additional revenues collected as a response to multilateral tax transparency initiatives that increase the global risk of detection of tax evasion, such as the CRS. In addition, the commencement of AEOI appears to have provided a significant boost to taxpayer responsiveness to domestic policy initiatives such as voluntary disclosure programmes, which have successfully encouraged evaders to declare non-compliant foreign accounts. In light of growing tax transparency, compliance of taxpayers, particularly among high-income earners, may thus continue to increase in the future.

Despite the progress made, further work is needed to tackle IFFs. All taxpayers need to pay their taxes where and when they are due and effective use of tax data and transmitted CRS information can help to achieve this aim by constantly increasing the risk of detection in case of non-compliance. The analysis suggests that matching CRS accounts with domestic tax records continues to be a challenge for South Africa. Moreover, South Africa's use of EOIR is more modest than some other African countries. Data exchanged under the CRS is being used for tax cases, but could be used also to assist in examining and analysing other kinds of financial crime.

Further strengthening tax capacity in South Africa is essential to ensuring that South Africa can make the most of EOI to address IFFs. Turning exchanged CRS information into an even more effective tool in the fight against tax evasion and IFFs requires further capacity building within tax authorities to comprehensively analyse taxpayer data, including by exchanging data with other agencies. Fostering inter-agency collaboration between authorities is necessary to exchange relevant information on a mutual basis and strengthen domestic enforcement, prosecution, and the possibility of asset recovery. Necessary cross-border information for this purpose is best obtained by increasing the number of actually exchanging AEOI partners and by more effectively using EOIR relationships, particularly with IFCs. These improvements will not only result in much needed additional revenue gains, but they will also increase the overall progressivity of the tax system and contribute to a more equal society.

Technical assistance can assist in expanding tax capacity. By providing technical assistance, the OECD through its Tax Inspectors Without Borders (TIWB) programme or regional initiatives such as the OECD Africa Academy for Tax and Financial Crime Investigation can assist in supporting countries in effectively implementing exchange of information and pursuing the impactful criminal investigation of financial crimes.

Meeting these targets sometimes reaches beyond the capacity of a single developing country and requires a strong collaborative effort with international partners. The present analysis is the first of its kind that conducts a targeted analysis of IFFs in an emerging economy through granular taxpayer and CRS data in close collaboration with national authorities. Further analysis could use a similar approach to analyse IFFs in other countries, or could deepen the analysis in South Africa through use of other data sources related to financial crime.

References

AU/ECA (2015), *Track it! Stop it! Get it! Report of the High Level Panel of Illicit Financial Flows from Africa*, https://repository.uneca.org/bitstream/handle/10855/22695/b11524868.pdf?sequence=3&isAllowed=y. [1]

Global Financial Integrity (2021), *Trade-Related Illicit Financial Flows in 134 Developing Countries: 2009-2018*, https://secureservercdn.net/50.62.198.97/34n.8bd.myftpupload.com/wp-content/uploads/2021/12/IFFs-Report-2021.pdf?time=1643653304. [2]

www.ingramcontent.com/pod-product-compliance
Ingram Content Group UK Ltd.
Pitfield, Milton Keynes, MK11 3LW, UK
UKHW050412240426
12048UKWH00020B/1480